Brenda DeVoe Marshall

*With Respect to
the Japanese*

The InterAct Series
Edited by
GEORGE W. RENWICK

Other books in the Series
AUSTRALIA/U.S.
GOOD NEIGHBORS: COMMUNICATING WITH THE MEXICANS
A COMMON CORE: THAIS AND AMERICANS
UNDERSTANDING ARABS

With Respect to the Japanese

A GUIDE FOR AMERICANS

JOHN C. CONDON

FOREWORD BY KOHEI GŌSHI

INTERCULTURAL PRESS INC.

Library of Congress Catalogue Card Number 81-85730
ISBN 0-933662-49-1

Printed in the United States of America

Contents

Preface

This is one of a series of books—the *InterAct* Series—which explains the interaction between Americans and people from other countries and cultures.

Unexpected difficulties (and opportunities) are encountered when people who have grown up in different cultures live, work and socialize together. Each *InterAct* book describes exactly what is encountered, why, and what to do about it. Readers discover what will embarrass, motivate, irritate and earn the respect of the foreign nationals with whom they are trying to communicate.

In this case—Japan—we are dealing, of course, with a critical trading and political partner. Our countries are linked almost inextricably in generating the economic and technical forces which shape the modern world. At the same time, the two countries are distant and the cultures are distinct. Experienced business personnel and diplomats in Japan and the U.S. have learned, sometimes through costly mistakes, that the road to success in working together lies, first, in careful study and real understanding of the values, priorities and practices of the other.

Knowing about the other, however, is not enough. Americans who know about Japan, even a lot about Japan, often do not know what happens when a Japanese and an American *come together* to transact business. Nor do they know how to carry this out effectively. In order to do so, and to accomplish their objectives, Americans must also know about their own culture and its strong influence upon them. Then they must know how—and when—to initiate, listen, clarify, persuade and collaborate. They must know, in other words, how to communicate. Cross-cultural communication, once regarded as a subject of interest only to scholars, is now in the headlines and boardrooms every day.

The author of this study, John C. Condon, lived and worked in Japan for ten years (throughout the 1970s). During this time he was a professor of communication at International Christian University. He conducted cross-cultural orientation and training for Japanese and American business organizations and government agencies, and lectured widely on intercultural communication. The influential "Pegasus Seminars," offered regularly by the American Chamber of Commerce in Japan and International House, were developed and directed by Dr. Condon. He is the author of a number of books including the highly respected *An Introduction to Intercultural Communication*.

Mr. Kyohei Gōshi, who kindly offered to write the Foreword to this book, is among the most famous and influential Japanese of this century. Along with men like Panasonic's Matsushita and Sony's Morita, Mr. Gōshi is known in his country as one of Japan's "Twelve Wise Men." He is the person perhaps most responsible for Japan's extraordinary productivity. For the past three decades, he has directed the landmark studies and training programs at the Japan Productivity Center which he founded.

Japanese values, techniques and products are having a great impact on American society. Similarly, what Americans want, how they think and why they behave as they do are of intense interest to the Japanese. Interaction is inevitable. *Successful* interaction, real communication, requires new insights and skills. Business personnel and diplomats must now develop intercultural competence.

We hope this book will enable Americans and Japanese to increase their competence and interact more successfully: as informed competitors or as compatible, productive partners.

George W. Renwick
Editor, *InterAct* Series

Foreword

I am pleased to say a few words at the beginning of Professor Condon's fine book on intercultural relations between Americans and Japanese. His understanding of our two cultures, and how we sometimes misunderstand each other because of our cultural differences, is very helpful. The book not only explains some of the differences in how people of Japan and the United States communicate, it also shows us ways in which we can avoid unnecessary misunderstandings and so cooperate together. In recent years, many articles and books have been written about problems of understanding between Japanese and Americans, but unfortunately very many have been superficial. I am very impressed with Professor Condon's research, perceptiveness and dedication to the improvement of understanding of both cultures, and I fully endorse what he presents here.

Cooperation is the key issue. For nearly thirty years we at the Japan Productivity Center have tried to encourage ways of cooperating among different interests within our own society as well as internationally. We have developed a model of cooperation that includes management, union representation, and a neutral party. In some ways this may be a very Japanese way of doing things. That is, as Professor Condon says in this book, "interpersonal harmony" rather than confrontation or starting from an adversary relationship, is a Japanese value. We have been gratified, therefore, that so many Americans in recent years have come to the Japan Productivity Center to learn from our experience. We have learned much from the Americans, and we believe that Americans may be able to learn something from us. Learning from each other, cooperating, we can each enjoy "a bigger piece of the pie."

Japanese people need to learn more about different cultural values and different ways of doing things. Our history shows us to be both a very special, unique culture, but also a culture that has a long tradition of learning from others. Sometimes in our history we have stressed our uniqueness, and sometimes we have stressed the value of learning from other cultures, East and West. Right now we are at a special time where we have a kind of balance between the two values. I hope it is not too bold to say that America, which has more often stressed its uniqueness and served as a teacher for other countries and cultures, is now much more open to learning from others. At least this is something we sense at the Japan Productivity Center. This is a very special time in this history of Japanese and American relations, as we both want to learn from each other.

There is one more theme that I would like to mention because I think it deserves more attention than it usually receives. That is the idea, or value, of respect. Without mutual respect, there cannot be long lasting communication nor true cooperation. We in our work at the Japan Productivity Center stress the importance of respect in increasing cooperation and thus increasing productivity. Respect is just as important in international and intercultural relations. It may be difficult to teach a person to respect another, unless we can help people to see things from the other's point of view. I hope that this book will help us increase our respect for the other by better understanding each other and by avoiding some of the common misunderstandings that often occur when people from Japan and the United States try to work together.

Kohei Gōshi
Founder and Chairman
The Japan Productivity Center
Tokyo

Introduction

Travel writers call almost any foreign country a "land of contrasts," but only Japan is so often called, by writers of all kinds, a "land of contradictions." *Time* magazine featured a cover story on Japan which explained to readers that "the Japanese have built their entire culture on contradictions." The cover itself reinforced that impression with a picture styled after an Edo era kabuki poster showing the hero in a defiant pose. This eighteenth century gentleman, however, carried in addition to his *bangasa* (paper umbrella), a pocket calculator, camera, digital watch, golf clubs, car keys and other modern day Japanese products that have helped to make SONY and Honda seem as American as pizza pie.

Even expatriate Americans long resident in Tokyo will tell newcomers, "If you plan to write about Japan, do so in the first four years. After that you'll know that whatever you say about Japan, the opposite can also be said." Such talk about contradictions may, however, only be a contemporary version of the "inscrutable" cliche Westerners used to apply to Asians generally. Such labeling does nothing to advance the understanding of another culture.

Contradictions exist in every society, but they are much more likely to be perceived from a distance than from within the culture. They are even more likely to reflect the outsider's expectations of what is consistent and what is contradictory, based on his own cultural background.

Americans, for example, are told by advertisers that new products are better than old ones. Given the American faith in technology and progress, it does not take much to persuade them. "Old" soon becomes "old fashioned" which becomes "obsolete." The ball point pen came to replace the fountain pen, and the xeroxing process seems to be doing away with carbon paper. These changes are expected. Americans are therefore surprised when they see in a modern Japanese bank or business office, employees using the *soroban* (abacus) as well as modern calculators. Another one of those Japanese contradictions? No, a Japanese will explain, for some things the *soroban* is just handier than a calculator. Each has its place. The same is true of those pens: in Japan the ball point pen has not exactly replaced the fountain pen any more than the fountain pen replaced the brush and *sumi* ink. Each has its place and continues to be used appropriately in Japan.

The American way of thinking resembles the logic of the sciences, where a new theory may replace the old. The Japanese way, in this case, is more like the logic of the arts: one may enjoy Bartok *and* Bach. Thus the Japanese "still" use chopsticks, "still" write Chinese characters, "still" want Shinto priests to consecrate the land for every new construction, including the new Tokyo Disneyland. The Americans still say "still."

American misunderstanding of Japan is partly the result of a lack of information and interest. Indeed Americans in general are much more "insular" in their knowledge of other places and peoples than are the Japanese. Harvard sociologist, Nathan Glazer, who has been monitoring reports and features about Japan for years, documents this. Even in the *New York Times,* the amount of information published during the years of Japan's greatest economic impact actually decreased. In 1972, the *Times* index showed a scant 2.6% of space devoted to Japan; six years later the percentage was only half of that.

As the 1980's began, however, there was a dramatic increase of interest in Japan. Book stores in America have whole sections devoted to books about Japan and about Japanese management in particular. William Ouchi's *Theory Z* even made the best seller list in 1982. Television specials on "how the Japanese get things done" have attracted large audiences. Seminars on QC's (quality circles) or Japanese management techniques or how to deal with the Japanese can now be found in large cities and college towns all over the United States. More and more Americans are sampling *sushi* and enjoying what they find, and learning to use *tofu* and other Japanese (albeit originally Chinese) food products.

The reasons for this surge of interest in Japan are perhaps more complex than they might appear. The economic success of the Japanese, which was related to effective marketing of quality products that were in demand in the States, was, of course, a major reason. But it was not just the SONY TV's and tape recorders, the Hondas, Datsuns, Toyotas and other vehicles, or the cameras and musical instruments. The Japanese in the United States, from Yoko Ono to Seiji Ozawa, seemed themselves to be "quality products."

The end of the seventies and the beginning of the eighties was not the first time Americans and Westerners took an interest in things Japanese; there were much earlier periods when Japan seemed fascinating and inspired works like *Madam Butterfly* and *The Mikado*. What was different this time was that thousands of Americans were meeting and working face-to-face with Japanese on matters of mutual interest on a daily basis.

Another reason lies with the Japanese themselves. Most Japanese seem to regard their culture as one that is extremely difficult for anyone but a Japanese to understand, and certainly not one into which an outsider could ever fit completely. In contrast to Americans, who believe that anyone could, and probably would if given half a chance, become an American, the Japanese find it hard to accept that anyone could become Japanese. This is reflected in everything from stringent government immigration policies to words of praise for the foreigner who can use chop sticks or sit for more than a few minutes on a *zabuton*. The newcomer is delighted by such compliments, but when the compliments continue after twenty years, the outsider knows that they carry an additional message.

In working with people from other cultures we stand a much better chance of understanding and learning to get along with them if we assume that each comes from a "land of consistency" rather than of contrasts and contradictions. And so it is with the Japanese. From generation to generation and from one area of activity to another the Japanese, with impressive consistency, behave very much like Japanese. Just as Americans behave like Americans.

With Respect to
the Japanese

1

The Odd Couple: America and Japan

An odd couple.

One is a central part of a continent that takes the names of two continents as its own. Richly endowed with natural resources, and with vast stretches of plains amenable to large scale farming, America produces food for the world. The other, the floating islands, is about the size of California and relatively lacking in resources. Mostly mountainous, with perhaps only a fifth of its land arable, nature is not always gentle. "Typhoon" is a Japanese word, as is *tsunami* (tidal-wave). And somewhere in Japan, however remote or minor, every few minutes there is an earthquake.

They are hemispheres apart, strikingly different in size and terrain, culturally distinct. The United States is "Western," and part of the new world. It is a nation whose peoples mark their history from a fixed date less than four centuries ago. The Japanese are Eastern and very old. They trace their history to a mythic past when gods and goddesses were upon the land. The legends say that Japan was born of bawdy laughter. It was the laughter of the gods who were watching a kind of strip-tease that coaxed Amaterasu-omikami, the Sun Goddess, from her cave where she had been sulking in darkness. Were it not for that there might be no Japan. America was founded upon rational principles and pragmatic expectations: a nation dedicated to a proposition, its credo written on paper and endorsed by its founders.

America was settled by Europeans—for the greater part of its short history, by immigrants from Britain and northern Europe. The native Americans, the "Indians," as the Europeans called all people who lived east of India, were excluded and displaced and made to feel alien in their own land. (In this regard, the Americans and the Japanese, in their treatment of the indigenous Ainu, have similar histories.) In time, this America, with its seemingly endless frontier containing room for all who wished to make something of their lives, became home for people from every part of the globe. The result is a people of striking ethnic diversity.

In this regard, no nation is more different from America than Japan. It is difficult to find on this earth a more homogeneous society, or one more exclusive. To be Japanese is to be born of Japanese parents, to look Japanese, to speak the Japanese language, and to act Japanese—the full set. Change any part and you spoil the symmetry, like a sour note in a sonata. Thus it is that Japanese often report their surprise, when visiting the U.S., that they are stopped by Americans and asked directions: "Can't they see that I am Japanese?" Americans assume that everybody, given the opportunity, will find hamburgers tasty, football exciting and jazz to their liking. Few Japanese expect outsiders to take to *onigiri* (rice balls), to thrill to *kendo* (traditional Japanese fencing), or to resonate with *enka* (that very Japanese genre of popular music in which female vocalists sing men's songs, and male vocalists sing what seem to be women's songs).

For all the borrowing from American and other Western cultures during the past century or so, the Japanese have retained a fairly clear distinction between what is traditionally Japanese and what is borrowed. These distinctions are reflected, for instance, in the use of words and in the writing system. All foreign and borrowed words—even the words for "glass" or "bread" which have been used in Japan longer than America has existed—are written in a syllabary which is different from the standard Japanese characters. It is as if every word that English could identify as derived from another language were italicized. Nor is it only native and borrowed words that are symbolically distinguished. Clothing, building design, foods are also divided symbolically. Thus the Japanese who excel in borrowing, adapting and, often, improving on what they borrow, are also skilled in keeping tabs on what is traditionally Japanese and what is not.

This is not to say that the Japanese are unfriendly to visitors or inhospitable to Americans or other Westerners who reside in Japan. Far from it. Few Americans who have visited Japan have failed to comment on the cordial and generous kindness of the Japanese. The difference is this: whereas an American might refer to someone who acts in ways quite different from those of most Americans as "a strange foreigner" in Japan the *hen na gaijin* (literally "strange foreigner") is the one who acts too much like a Japanese.

In matters of the spirit, the distance between the two is even more apparent. Americans draw upon the Judeo-Christian tradition (originated in the East) which, giving credit to their consistency, they have tried to keep separate from matters of State. Still, few countries in modern times have sent more missionaries abroad to spread religious "truth" than the U.S. Most Americans claim allegiance to an organized religion. Ask any ten Japanese about their religious beliefs, on the other hand, and nine will likely answer that they have none. But nearly all will have been blessed at a Shinto shrine in their infancy and nearly all will depart this earth guided by Buddhist priests. Japanese foods and festivals exude Shintoism, its arts and aesthetics Buddhism. Perhaps one percent of the Japanese belong to Christian sects.

There are, of course, similarities which are not to be ignored. Both societies have a comparable high regard for such qualities as honesty, cleanliness, efficiency. Both enjoy a congenial technology and delight in what is new. Both have a strong middle class, both value formal education, both are democracies with reasonably well informed and responsive electorates. Such a list could be expanded considerably, particularly in outward forms such as the shape of modern buildings or design of clothing, which are almost identical in the big cities of Japan and the U.S. But where the inner life is concerned—that which has been shaped by culture—fundamental differences are revealed. The most serious mistake Americans can make when interacting with Japanese is to be insensitive to these differences because Japan seems to be "Westernized" in its current affluent and technologically advanced state. Japanese are not likely to confuse the outward appearances with the inner reality. On the contrary, the most serious mistake many Japanese make, in the opinion of some Americans, is to ignore some similarities because of the overriding faith that things Japanese must be unique.

2

The Cultural Mold:
Differences that Make a Difference

A newcomer to Japan asked an American consultant who had been in Japan more than a decade if the increasing similarities between Japanese and Western ways weren't beginning to outweigh the differences. The consultant replied.

"In my experience, the outward similarities just make the subtle differences more difficult to recognize, and therefore even more important, the problem is that the typical American only notices the obvious differences—driving on the left or some guy in a tuxedo taking a leak at the side of the road in the middle of the city. The most important differences are the ones that really make a difference when Japanese and Americans or other foreigners try to work together."

How does one find these differences that make a difference?

5

According to our consultant:

> "Rule one: if you notice a difference, realize that difference in itself may not be so important. It's what you don't notice that counts. Rule two: in almost everything in Japan there is some unseen or unstated meaning which is usually not pointed out but which everybody is supposed to know. So my advice is to look for the underlying meanings.
>
> A lot of businessmen coming over here these days make the mistake of only focusing on management practices or some other aspect of business, and always comparing them with what Americans would do. My advice is to look for some of the subtle differences in the ways things are done when you don't expect to see any differences. Look at business practices, sure, but also look at what people do at parties, how people talk to each other, and how kids are taught. You'll find some basic differences that make a difference."

A fascinating study conducted a few years ago makes this point precisely. A team of Japanese and American researchers visited several kindergartens in Japan. These included American schools and international schools strongly influenced by Americans (in staffing, language used and enrollment). Others were *yochien,* Japanese kindergartens. The researchers were interested in children's drawings. They wondered if, given the same instructions, the children from the two cultures would produce significantly different pictures. If Henry drew a picture of the sun, for example, would he color it yellow while Hiroshi's sun would be colored red, just like the sun in his country's flag? The answer, as it turned out, was a resounding yes, so much so that almost anybody could sort through the hundred odd drawings and nearly always guess which were done by Japanese children and which were drawn by Americans.

But as culture is more a process than its products, more an event than an object, the truly revealing differences appeared in *how* the children made their pictures. If we take a closer look at what happened when these children were asked to "draw a picture of your family," we can learn a good deal about Japanese and American ways of looking at the world and doing things. We can also anticipate some of the problems that can result when people from both cultures attempt to work together.

To begin with, the seating arrangements in each school were different. In some American classrooms there were individual desks, while in others the children sat on the floor. In all of the Japanese kindergartens, however, the children sat around tables in groups of six or eight. Each group had its own name such as that of a flower or bird and this group served as the basic unit for many of the children's activities.

The roles of the teachers were also different. When the researchers visited a school to ask the children to draw the pictures, the American teachers invited the visitors to "go right ahead and tell the boys and girls what you want them to do." In the Japanese schools, however, all communication was handled by the teacher. She remained the authority, the responsible person and "go-between."

How the children began and how they carried out the activity also differed. Usually, as soon as an American child received a sheet of paper he or she would begin to draw. When the picture was finished, the child would hold it up to be collected or would bring it to the teacher's desk. In the Japanese schools the children waited until all of the papers had been distributed. Then, at each table, the children looked at each other and talked a little about what they were supposed to do. Then, table by table, as if by signal, all the children would begin to draw. Throughout the activity, children would turn and look at what the others were doing. Those who finished first waited until the others were done, and when all were finished the drawings were collected.

When children showed difficulty in drawing someone in the family, the responses of the teachers were also different. The Japanese teacher would usually assist the child, not infrequently taking the child's hand and guiding the crayon. (This is truly "hands-on-learning"! It is the same method used to teach Japanese children other skills such as writing and bowing.) In the American schools, the teachers encouraged the children in words: "Just do your best." "It's *your* father and *your* picture and *you* should try to draw him the way *you* see him."

Finally, the order in which the family members were drawn was also notably different. For the Japanese youngsters, the order usually began with father, then mother, then older brother or sister. The child would draw himself or herself next, and if there were still younger ones, they would be drawn last. For the American children the order seemed much more random. The only notable tendency was for some children to draw themselves first.

In short, there were cultural differences in the physical arrangements of the rooms, the kind of contact with an outsider that was allowed, the extent of coordination in the beginning and ending of tasks, the role of the person in charge of the activity and the kind of instruction that person offered, and the depiction of social relationships, "the social order." Each of these themes is worth a closer look, for together with other themes, they characterize some of the major features that contrast the two societies and are at the heart of many of the confusions and conflicts that arise when Japanese and Americans work together.

Individual or Group: "I" or "We"

Every person, everywhere, is both an individual, separate from others, and also a member of a group, emotionally tied to others. Cultural background influences which of these characteristics—the independent individual or the interdependent group member—is given emphasis when we think of ourselves. Japan and the U.S. differ sharply in this regard.

In countless ways, both obvious and subtle, the Japanese are encouraged to think first of being part of the group. "We" always comes before "I." *We* of this family, *we* of this nation, or just *"we"* who are together in a room talking. One is never fully independent; one must always be conscious of others. (An American teacher in Japan remarked, "If Descartes had been Japanese, he would have said 'we think, therefore we are.'")

For Americans the individual, not the group, is basic. So many of the values Americans hold dear—equality, democracy, freedom, privacy, and even progress are bound up with the American view of individualism. Cooperation and teamwork are important, to be sure, but these should arise from the choice and desire of the individual.

These are not simply interesting cultural differences. They are very emotional issues. Americans can become upset when a Japanese expresses an opinion beginning with *"Wareware nihonjin"* ("We Japanese"). "Just give me *your own* opinion," the American may insist. Likewise Japanese find some expressions of American individualism rude and anti-social. Americans tend to speak in terms of "my opinion," and "I think," and so on, in order to be both personal and also cautious about speaking for others. Nevertheless, the impression given can be one of egotism. A similar problem occurs when an American chimes in to help complete the sentence of a Japanese. Very often the American is simply trying to show that he is listening attentively and understands. The Japanese may find this arrogant and overbearing.

Here are some of the ways in which Japanese emphasize the "we" over the "I":

Hiring Practices

Japanese employees are hired as a group or "class," once a year, much like students entering a school. Though their activities may differ, they work together, eat together, and many will live together in a company dormitory. The ability to get along with others is therefore a very important criterion for being hired. Character, along with family background and school attended, usually count for much more than specialized training or outstanding personal abilities, for these could work against one's ability to fit in comfortably. A Japanese-American was being interviewed for a position with a major Japanese corporation known throughout the world. The student had lived in Japan many years and was fluent in both English and Japanese. Each of the persons who interviewed the candidate was apparently most concerned about his American background, for each stressed "there is no room for individualism in this company."

Another young employee of a prestigious trading company became disillusioned with company policies after about one year. He was an idealist and some of what went on did not meet his ideals. He considered what few Japanese fortunate enough to work for the company would have contemplated: leaving the company and perhaps returning to graduate school and then going into teaching. He sought advice from many persons, and finally decided to remain. What most persuaded him to stay? "I realized," he told this writer with whom he had studied in college, "that if I left the company, it would make it much more difficult for others from this college to be hired by the company in the future."

Decision-making

In most cases, Japanese prefer decision by consensus rather than by vote. People should talk and talk until some agreement emerges. If the mood is such that no consensus seems possible, then it may be best to defer making a decision. Though Americans may not be unhappy to reach consensus, voting is a part of the American way—even in schoolrooms and in homes. One person, one vote: this preserves the rights of the individual. Americans believe people should "stand up and be counted." An old Japanese saying represents another point of view: "The nail that stands up will be pounded down."

Language

Two of the most frequently used words in English are "I" and "you." It is difficult to talk very long without using these pronouns many times in many ways, but always independently: I am *I* no matter who you are, and you are *you* no matter who I am. It doesn't matter if the two people talking are of the same sex or not, the same age or not, or if they have just met or are old friends. Not so in Japanese. There are at least ten words in Japanese that might be equivalent to the English "I," and another ten for "you" depending upon a particular relationship. Relative age, status, role, familiarity with each other, whether or not both are men or both women or man and woman together will all influence how Japanese talk. It is not just the pronouns that are truly relative; other features of speaking are also adjusted. This is why some Japanese say that they "feel more individualistic" when speaking English and why for no-nonsense talk English is a far better language than Japanese, at least from the point of view of many Japanese. "English is a perfect language for lawyers," said one Japanese friend, "but not for gently getting to know each other. English is like algebra—hypothetical, impersonal, practical, modern, direct, whatever. It's easy to say 'yes' or 'no' in English. That's what I like about it, it makes sense, is so modern."

Nonverbal Expressions

The attention given to relationships applies to other forms of communicating too, such as bowing when greeting or departing. An American handshake does not indicate much about the relationship between the two people, who is older or of higher status, for example. In Japan, however, relationships are clearly shown in the bow—even if accompanied by a handshake as sometimes happens today. As we will discuss later, younger bows lower than older, lower status person bows lower than higher status person, and so on.

Clothing in Japan reflects the individual's relationship to the group much more than is so in the States. Japan is a nation of uniforms, not just for mail carriers, clerks and clergy but for students, housewives, business people, entertainers and vacationers. (Guests who stay at a hot springs resort will don the hotel's *yukata*, a lightweight kimono, so that even while strolling about town, others can immediately identify who "belongs" to which resort hotel.) There is even a kind of appropriate dress for newlyweds.

Most of these uniforms are by no means official, but it is not so difficult for an alert Japanese to pick out on a crowded commuter train who is who on the basis of how each is dressed. Many companies have standard dress policies or uniforms. At the SONY offices and plants in Japan there is a standard smock which everybody, factory worker and President alike, wears. At SONY's large plant in San Diego, on the other hand, American employees objected to having to dress alike at work and so the company gave up the "dress code" at that location.

3

Harmony in Interpersonal Relations

If one identifies strongly with a group, it is especially important to maintain good relations and avoid conflicts with others in the group. Even away from the group, the family, school or business, one must be careful not to act in such a way that might cause embarrassment to the group.

Moreover, in Japan, school loyalties and company employment last a very long time. Transferring from school to school or company to company is uncommon. To want to change suggests that the person may not have been able to get along well with others and raises questions about how well the person can fit into the new situation. Changing is also discouraged because the person who enters laterally simply will not be able to draw from experiences shared with others who have been together for a longer time. Changing one's affiliation from one school to another or from one company to another is perceived as disruptive; it doesn't contribute to the harmony of the group.

Efforts to maintain harmony are reflected in many ways including cautious and indirect speech, taking time to sense another's mood before venturing an opinion, and avoiding as much as possible public disagreement. The experience in the Japanese kindergarten also showed two other important means of ensuring harmony: the use of a go-between and the coordination of actions.

The Go-Between

When the teacher acted as a buffer between the children in class and the visitors, she served a basic function of a go-between: to deflect direct contact between people which might otherwise be awkward, confusing or disruptive. In any enterprise of importance, be it a marriage or a business venture, the go-between in Japan plays a prominent role. He or she provides background information for both parties, attempts to set the right mood for the first meeting, and ensures that the parties are serious and sincere. If things do not go well, then the go-between can soften the bad news and lessen the disappointment. If a union is made, then the go-between remains a human bond in the contract. To dissolve that union, whether a marriage or a business partnership, is also to involve the go-between, and thus there is extra pressure for people to resolve disputes.

Americans also use contacts, third parties as mediators and such, but the preference is for directness. "Speak for yourself, John." Or as the kindergarten teacher told the visitors, "Go ahead and tell the kids what you want them to do." In working with the Japanese, Americans often appear too direct: they are likely to leave out the middleman or fail to go through the proper channels. Sometimes this is because Americans in

Japan do not know who to involve or how to proceed. In many cases, however, there is a cultural reason for wanting to get on with things and not waste time. As it so often turns out, however, the direct approach in Japan is the least efficient. In Japan the shortest distance between two points is a curved line.

There is one kind of third party which Americans involve much more than the Japanese: the lawyer. The lawyer's role, in fact, is partly to aid the directness Americans prefer by putting things in writing in a language that should make it clear where each side stands. American contracts are usually very detailed and make explicit agreements, intentions and consequences. Japanese contracts seem by comparison to be general and vague. America also has many times the number of lawyers that Japan has, at least partly because Japanese disputes are usually settled out of court. The lawyer in Japan is normally called in only when problems have reached a crisis stage. "When a lawyer shows up," a perceptive observer once remarked, "it is like the appearance of a Buddhist priest who is called in to administer the last rites."

Beginnings and Endings

Another visible expression of harmony in the kindergarten was the way the children began and concluded their work together. To start before others or to turn in one's work while others are still working sets one apart. It may also suggest that the person is rude, selfish or not well brought up. Such an attitude is not unknown to Americans, but Americans are more likely to associate beginning and ending as a group with a formal occasion such as a religious service or formal dinner. And Americans say they prefer informality.

Japanese have many everyday expressions to announce the beginning and endings of activities. There are set expressions in Japanese for when one leaves the house and when one returns, when one begins a meal and when one is finished. Bus drivers may announce when the bus is starting and when it is stopping, and television announcers will state that the program has begun and that it has come to an end. Such expressions always relate the individual to the group or help synchronize group activities. Department stores begin each day with a formal opening; chimes ring out, uniformed attendants swing open the doors, and the personnel in every section bow to the first arriving customers and bid them welcome. At closing time, it is the tune of "Auld Lang Syne" that announces the store or restaurant or bar is closing.

Group synchrony is enhanced in other ways, too—frequent meetings at work, dining and drinking with co-workers after hours, college dorm meetings. Sometimes Americans regard these as "ritualistic" and hence a waste of time. American students studying in Japan have been known to stop attending dorm or club meetings or come but then leave early because they have a test to study for or a paper to complete. Japanese students regard such behavior as selfish or "too individualistic." The same kind of behavior and judgment can be seen in tour groups with Americans—and Westerners generally—not wanting to have to do what everyone else does and wanting to go off on their own. When this happens in Japan, there can be problems. "They should at least inform the leader," a Japanese guide complained, "since the leader is the officially responsible person." The American reaction: "Inform the leader? I'm an adult, and I can take care of myself. I shouldn't have to ask permission!"

One other scene of coordination, even synchrony, can be observed each morning in factory yards, schools, and high above the ground in modern office buildings. This is the sight of Japanese doing group calisthenics. "*Ichi, ni, – san, shi. . .*" the radio exercise instructor calls out to the familiar radio exercise tune, as everybody bends and stretches in harmony.

Beginning together, ending together, every day much of the nation from Hokkaido to Okinawa literally moves together in harmony. For most Americans that is an unattractive image—"regimented," "militaristic," "ant-like."

The Way

The Japanese teacher's direct guidance of the child's drawing, in contrast to the American's encouragement to "draw your picture the way you want it," suggests another important part of Japanese life: learning the proper form.

The suffix "*-do*" as in *judo, kendo, bushido* means "the *way*," but the idea of a correct "way" extends far beyond traditional martial arts or flower arranging or calligraphy in Japan. There is a *right way* to exchange condolences, a *right way* to greet one's superior and a *right way* to greet the new year, and a *right way* to offer a drink, accept a gift and decline a compliment. The way to learn *the way*, of course, is to be taught by those who are older and wiser, more experienced. One's elders and superiors command respect in part because they know a lot.

Americans and others who work with Japanese sometimes underestimate the value placed on doing things "right." It is not so much that what is done is difficult to learn—exchanging business cards, for example. The problem is that for many Americans, *how* one does something doesn't seem all that important. The overseas businessperson, exchange student or tourist may say, "Oh, what difference does it make?" meaning they can't see any importance in how such simple, everyday actions are performed. In Japan, however, these matters are very important for they reflect upon one's upbringing, character and even one's sincerity in a particular situation. They also reflect on one's group. There are some parallels in the U.S. when Americans display good manners by arranging for no interruptions while meeting with a colleague during office hours or by saying the appropriate thing when offering condolences or congratulations but rather than following "the way," one selects from an array of "acceptable ways" that have been learned more often by observation and trial than by explicit instruction.

Take the example of the *meishi* (business card) exchange, an act performed maybe a million times every day in Japan. Because the card represents one's organization, the cards must be exchanged with all due respect. One receives another's card as one might a token gift, with thanks and appreciation. One should look at the card carefully and perhaps make some comment which serves to acknowledge receiving it. The card will then be carefully put aside for future reference; after the other party leaves, the recipient may write a note on the card to help him remember something about the meeting in the future. (Most Japanese will keep these cards in a special file just for such purposes.) When presented, the cards are not to be dealt out like playing cards on a table or received and stuffed into a wallet and sat upon. The visitor who handles a card with little respect presents a poor image of himself and of the organization that chose to hire him.

This does not mean that the Japanese expect foreigners to try to act like the Japanese. Quite the contrary. In Japan, remember, *hen na gaijin*, the "strange foreigner," is one who overdoes things, who tries, by Japanese standards, to "go native." A Japanese business consultant gave this advice:

> "There are many things you should try to do properly when you are in Japan, but the Japanese do not expect you to do everything we do. You should try to know what the Japanese regard as the proper way, and then adjust accordingly."

This is very good advice. Try to learn what the Japanese regard as "the proper way" of doing all sorts of things that might strike you, as an outsider, as unimportant or unnecessary, whether it is an act as simple and automatic as serving tea to any guest who arrives whether or not they are thirsty, or something more subtle as how to receive a gift or decline a compliment. Americans who ignore the little courtesies of custom and culture may publicly explain that they don't want to appear to be mimicking the Japanese for fear they will seem to be "going native," but the real reason, in this writer's opinion, is their fear of seeming clumsy or foolish. Americans seem to think that if they try something and do not act quite right, they will be noticed and criticized but if they just "act like themselves" they will be either ignored or excused. This is not an assumption Americans grant to people from other cultures when they are in the States. The better assumption is just the opposite: try to do what seems appropriate and expected and you will either be ignored because your actions seem so "natural" or, if not quite right, will still be at least appreciated and admired because you made the effort. As one Japanese journalist put it:

> "Foreigners in Japan should avoid the extremes of adjustment—not trying at all or trying too much. If they make no effort to adjust to Japanese ways, they are simply tolerated. If they are like Japanese in every way except for appearance, they are regarded as strange—unless their background is known, such as *gaijin* who grew up in Japan. Foreigners working in Japan are at their best when they 'behave with an accent.'"

The Social Order

The aspect of Japanese culture which is probably the most subject to misinterpretation and which provokes the strongest emotional response from Americans is the hierarchical nature of the social structure. The Japanese are extremely status conscious. When the Japanese children drew their families beginning with the father and ending with the youngest child, they were demonstrating why social scientists often call Japan a "vertical society."

There are many ways in which the Japanese publicly acknowledge a social hierarchy—in the use of language, in seating arrangements at social gatherings, in bowing to one another and hundreds of others. Watch Japanese greet each other and the principles will become quite apparent. Notice who bows lower, who waits for the other to go first, who apologizes more: (1) younger defers to older; (2) female defers to male; (3) student defers to teacher; (4) the seller's bow is lower than the buyer's; and (6) in a school club or organization where ranks are fixed, the lower ranked is, of course, subordinate.

All of this can be a source of irritation for many Americans. For one thing, the very words used in attempting to describe the patterns are emotionally loaded: "superior," "subordinate," or worse yet, "inferior." Moreover, Americans usually infer that if differences are stressed, then one must always be *better* than the other. In a word: discrimination. Understanding is further complicated because, as some Japanese scholars have argued in recent years, the "horizontal" in Japanese human relations is also important but has been overlooked, just as the "vertical" in American society tends to be ignored because it is not part of the American value system. (American women, like Japanese women, also smile more than men, take up less space than men, are interrupted more by men and interrupt men less in conversation, and so on.) A Japanese high school exchange student was shocked by what she called "the feudal system" in American high school sports activities. "The coach is some teacher who comes in and tells students what to do. In Japanese high school sports activities, the student or former students run things. They do everything they demand others to do. Japan is a lot more democratic," she felt.

In business and industry the much vaunted Japanese productivity is related at least as much to horizontal networks as to the vertical structure. The QC (Quality Circle) groups of workers who meet regularly to discuss ways of improving the means of production or the product itself are people of equal rank in the hierarchy, motivated from within rather than ordered from above. Though the QC can be regarded as an American innovation, the fact remains that it has taken hold in Japan in a way it never did in the States.

Then, too, there is the question of what transpires up and down the vertical line. American management is generally characterized as "top down" management, with plans and procedures determined at the top and implemented down the line. Japanese management gives much more authority and responsibility to those in lower ranking positions, so that sometimes the manager's function is merely to endorse what has come up the line. This is the *ringi* system, which has attracted so much interest among American managers in recent years.

Nevertheless, many Westerners perceive yet another Japanese contradiction in the public hierarchy: an antiquated social system in an otherwise modern industrialized nation. ". . . There has been little change in the way Japanese men treat women since the days of Confucius," begins an article on Japanese women in an issue of the American magazine, *Executive Female*. There are serious inequities in Japanese society and these are criticized strongly by Japanese women and men. But Japanese women are understandably annoyed when American women set about to "liberate our sisters." Said one young Japanese woman, "I would rather be treated in a patronizing way by Japanese men than in a matronizing way by American women."

Each system must be viewed on its own terms, and not on the expectations of the other. In the case of deference due to age, for example, not only the social system but the language, aesthetic sensitivity, and religious outlook reflect the same respect for the old. The Japanese language has no single word for brother, for example; one must choose between a word meaning "older brother" and one meaning "younger brother." The same is true for sister. Moreover, in the family the older brothers and sisters will be called by those terms, rather than by their given names. Being older does not, however, mean that one can do what one pleases. Older brother or older sister has special responsibilities toward parents and toward younger ones. Being older is not necessarily an enviable position. The younger is able to depend upon and lean on the older for support, a pattern that holds true among school mates of different ages as well. This is the *sempai-kohai* (senior-junior) bond which continues long after college and extends into the business world with favors sought and granted between the former students who are bound together because of—not in spite of—their differences in age.

Being sensitive to one's age or seniority in an organization relative to someone else gives a person a sense of security and guides how one communicates with others. Because of the hiring practices mentioned before and the expectation of "life-time employment," there is usually a parallel between age and rank. A younger person may be more able than an older person, and everybody may recognize that, but the younger will still show deference to the older.

In the case of a Japanese student and teacher, the student bows to his teacher at school and on the street out of respect for the role of teachers and respect for education in the society. Years later, if that former student should become, say, Prime Minister, and if he should again meet his old teacher on the street, the student will still bow low to his teacher. It is not a matter of who is more famous or powerful. It is a matter of acknowledging one's proper place in a system that helps to maintain reasonably harmonious human relations in a crowded land.

In intercultural encounters, however, things can get mixed up. A fifty-nine year old Japanese vice president of a Japanese bank may meet to discuss something with an American vice president of the Tokyo branch of an American bank and find that the American is only thirty-nine years old. When they meet, should their bowing reflect their different ages or their identical rank? Will the Japanese vice president have any misgivings about an American organization that sends such a young representative? Does the difference in age reflect the American hierarchy of branches and affiliates? This is the stuff of diplomacy. It should be pointed out that some of the awkwardness in such a situation is reduced if the two converse in English, which requires less fine tuning to fit each social situation than does Japanese.

Social Reciprocity

Social reciprocity, or the "give and take" in everyday life, is important in all societies. Americans may wonder about the person who is sent a Christmas card but never writes back, or may keep track of who owes who lunch or a favor. Generally speaking, though, Americans have a fairly loose attitude toward social debts and favors. The Japanese, on the other hand, have a very keen sense of reciprocity and all that it might imply. Misunderstanding and irritation about how this operates and its importance frequently occur in American-Japanese relations as a result.

The old expression "one good turn deserves another" is a rule that should be adhered to in Japan. If Mr. Suzuki asks a favor from Mr. Ohno, he does so with a strong feeling of obligation to repay the favor as precisely and as soon as possible. Mr. Ohno, for his part, knows that Mr. Suzuki feels this way. Similarly, if Mr. Suzuki offers something to Mr. Ohno, he does so knowing that Mr. Ohno will feel obligated to return something in kind. Thus, it is that Japanese enter into relationships with caution—whether the relationships be between individuals or corporations—for the feeling of beginning a series of never ending reciprocal exchanges is very strong indeed.

Consider the variety of such exchanges. A woman gives a plate of sweets she has made to the woman next door; soon, pushed by cultural expectations and not personal inclinations or convenience, the neighbor will return the plate—with some other morsel set upon it, or if there is nothing, with at least a sheet of paper to serve as a token return gift. Any person invited to a wedding in Japan is obliged to give a gift, with money being especially appreciated. Each guest at the wedding reception, upon leaving, will in turn be given a gift from the wedding couple. Even at funerals, where gifts (money presented in a special envelope) are usually given, those who have paid their respects will likely be given some small appropriate gift in return.

Visitors to Japan are often surprised by the number of snapshots taken. Most of these are to be sent to people who have visited. If the visitor has taken similar pictures, it is a good idea to send copies to Japanese hosts or friends. For Americans this might be a "nice thought" or a "considerate gesture," something "personal." For the Japanese it is assumed, expected, so that the failure to meet this expectation becomes the more personal (or "American!"). The Japanese have institutionalized thoughtfulness—and it works.

Even at a meal this kind of exchange is apparent. One should not pour sake or even beer for oneself—unless dining alone or with family. One always pours for the other, and that person will hold or touch the cup or glass as it is filled, to acknowledge the act. The process is then reversed, each pouring for the other in exchange. With sake cups so small, the number of exchanges can be many, and the sense of social ties repeatedly expressed and strengthened. Business debts are not so different. One enters into a relationship cautiously but is then careful to maintain the balance.

Double Standards

Some years ago the noted Japanese anthropologist Chie Nakane was quoted by a reporter as saying "the Japanese have no principles." Taken out of context that seems a terrible thing to say about any people. What Professor Nakane was referring to, however, is an important distinction between Japanese and Americans, and is at the base of some serious misinterpretations across cultures.

Americans pride themselves on being people of principle, even if they do not always live up to those principles. Americans would like the same principles to apply to all people in all situations; Americans resent "double standards." Americans also feel that a person of principle should stick up for what he believes instead of saying one thing while thinking another. At the same time, Americans do consider it a virtue to be "diplomatic" and avoid unnecessarily hurting or upsetting others.

Japanese are, it has been said, extremely sensitive to situations, to doing or saying what is appropriate in a particular circumstance. The Japanese do not expect all people to be treated in the same way in all situations, nor do they think it is wise to always speak out what one believes. From a Japanese point of view this is not a matter of hypocrisy or deviousness. Rather it is a recognition that a kind of "double standard" is necessary and practical.

The Japanese use the terms *tatemae* and *honne* to describe these two standards which work in parallel, not in conflict. *Tatemae* is literally the outward structure of a building; the term refers to what is outwardly expressed, what appears on the surface. *Honne* is literally one's "true voice," and it refers to what one really thinks or feels. The Japanese assume that there may be a difference between what one says and what one thinks. How else could it be in a society that values harmony in interpersonal relations, that discourages individualistic outspokenness, and that restrains the bold expression of personal feelings.

The effects of this difference in "standards" are many. Japanese are more likely to take into account the circumstances in which something is expressed and judge accordingly how much reflects *honne* and how much is *tatemae*. Americans are more likely to want to take words at face value. Moreover, if there is a difference in what is said and what is felt and that difference becomes apparent, Americans may be quite critical. Japanese, on the other hand, may sympathize with a person who is put into a situation where it is difficult for that person to say what he or she is thinking.

Some years ago this writer directed a study of ways Japanese use to avoid having to say "no" in Japan. Some sixteen frequently used ways were identified, each of which was appropriate for certain situations. Some of the ways are by no means unknown to Americans, such as giving an ambiguous answer, but others are more "Japanesey"—such as saying "yes" to mean no![1]

Americans are well advised to always consider the circumstances in which something is said. While this may also be good advice within America, the occasions, settings, "contexts" in Japan generally exert much more influence on what is said or not said than is the case for Americans. Often circumstances dictate whether one can reveal one's "true voice,"

[1] Masaaki Imai, President of the Cambridge Corporation in Tokyo, wrote a delightful guide for Americans working with Japanese, the title of which says it so clearly: *Never Take Yes For An Answer* (Tokyo: Simul Press, 1973).

or say what he is expected or constrained to say. One's true voice can be heard in a situation that allows for it. This is one reason the informal, after hours, settings for gathering with co-workers is so important in Japan. For the same reasons, Americans should take care not to ask blunt questions in situations where the Japanese would find it difficult to respond frankly.

Americans worry that they get "too much *tatemae*" from the Japanese and not enough *honne*. "It's a lot harder to know what my Japanese staff members are thinking than with people from any other culture I've worked with," said one business executive with considerable overseas experience. Japanese, on the other hand, are sometimes irked by what they feel is an American habit to express a "true voice" in situations where more "*tatemae*" is called for—as in some formal settings or in staff sessions with the top officials of the organization.

But there is more to this than an imbalance of courtesy and candor. There is a kind of American style of "*tatemae*" which Japanese sometimes interpret as "*honne*." A Japanese engineer, transferred to the American home office, was at first confused then upset when Americans, seeming outwardly so friendly, would make vague overtures of invitations to dinner but never follow through. Later, he philosophized:

> "Americans think we Japanese are too polite for too long—but it takes a long time for Japanese to become real friends. But Americans, I think, seem too friendly too soon, so we Japanese don't know if they are really friendly or just being polite American style."

One other "double standard" that should be mentioned is the distinction between *uchi,* literally the "house," and *soto,* literally the "outside." Japanese mark a much clearer distinction between what pertains to the family or school group or company, etc., (the "house"), and matters that are outside of those domains. Thus behavior that is appropriate within one's group may be expected to be different from behavior that is appropriate with people outside of one's group. The double standard is expected. Moreover, when Japanese represent their *uchi,* their company, say, their behavior conforms to standards that may be quite different from the standards appropriate for when one is simply another stranger in a crowd. So it is that the Japanese gentleman who in one situation seems exceedingly polite is later seen rudely forcing his way into some crowded department store elevator. Americans are more likely to expect consistent behavior, irrespective of circumstances. Japanese express surprise that Americans will often say thank you to, for instance, a cashier when receiving change.

Because the distinction between *uchi* and *soto* is so important, Japanese are very careful about who they let into "the house"—that is, who is hired by the company or who is admitted to the university or, of course, who is admitted into the family by marriage. Once admitted, however, the person becomes part of "us" and is not likely to be dismissed. Students in Japan rarely flunk out of universities. The expectation for employees when hired is that they will remain with the company until retirement.

Americans in most instances do not value such a clear separation, nor do they value the difficulty of entering and the expectation of remaining within groups and organizations. It is much easier for Americans to enter, leave, and move about from school to school, company to company, and increasingly from one marital relationship to another. This allows more freedom for the individual, which is so valued, and it seems, at least from the American perspective, more democratic than does the Japanese way.

Americans who have lived in Japan for some time frequently complain that the Japanese are exclusive, meaning that Americans will sometimes be excluded from entering certain places or organizations. Japanese friends do not extend invitations to their homes. There are certain "Japanese only" bars, American reporters are not allowed into Japanese press conferences, Japanese immigration laws are exclusionary. "The house," in each case, is different with different traditions, demands, expectations. But consistently there is the assumption that whoever is admitted must be like "us," must be expected to act as we would act, to fit in and not, whether intended or not, to stand out. Not many Americans—or others from "the outside"—are prepared to conform to those expectations.

Face

Americans who have had little contact with Japanese are likely to wonder about the concept of "face," which they have heard is extremely important to Japanese (as well as many other Asian peoples). Is "face" comparable to what Americans might call "reputation" or "image"? Is the concern to save face and not to "lose face" a kind of cultural neurosis, an exaggerated worry about what others think, rather than something more tangible? Or, as one American put it, "Americans and Asians see things in anatomical opposites; they save face, we cover our ass!" (In fact, the expressions to "lose face" or "save face" are more Chinese than Japanese; the comparable Japanese concern is expressed in terms of getting one's face dirtied or muddied, rather than losing face.)

The difficulty Americans have in understanding "face" in Japan stems largely from the emphasis placed by American values on the individual. The Japanese, in contrast, emphasize the group—the family, school, company, etc.—of which the individual is a part. From the Japanese perspective, therefore, how one treats others and is treated by them is of supreme importance, and so to slight another or to feel slighted, to cause embarrassment or be embarrassed, disturbs the delicate web of relationships which are essential to survival. What others think of a person really does matter in Japan.

The word "face" expresses very well this sense of how someone is seen or sees another. The Japanese mother teaches her child not to do or say certain things "or else people will laugh at you." This is a concern for face and appeals to the primary means of social control in the culture, shame. Japan is often identified as a "shame culture," where proper behavior is ensured through outside social pressure. This contrasts with the kind of controls identified with American, and Western societies generally, where it is the internal feelings, guilt, that are said to guide behavior. This is the matter of "conscience," or of being "God fearing." This well known distinction between shame cultures and guilt cultures is, of course, not so clear cut. Americans can be very sensitive to what others say and think, and Japanese can be guided by an inner gyroscope that seems inalterable in the face of adversity. Nevertheless, concern for what others think, most importantly those others who constitute one's group, is a basic value and fact of life in Japan. (Suicide in Japan, often misunderstood in America, is the ultimate means of taking responsibility for having brought shame to one's group. This most personal act is, in Japan, still an act that expresses a supreme concern for what others think.)

A person who is embarrassed in public—that is, in such a way that others become aware of it—shares that embarrassment with those of his group. A child who is disgraceful to his teacher brings shame on the child's family as well as on himself. A businessman or government official who is embarrassed because he, or those for whom he is responsible, are shown to be incompetent or dishonest brings shame upon his group. That is why Japanese caught in such situations are much more likely to offer their resignations immediately rather than to fight things out. Taking full responsibility, particularly on the part of the person who is officially responsible, removes the burden that would otherwise have to be shared by others.

Shame is also used calculatingly to exert pressure. It sometimes happens that an employee who might in the States be fired is, in Japan, simply given no more work to do. As a result he may come to the office and have nothing to occupy his time except reading the newspaper while his colleagues continue to work away. Soon enough the feeling of shame will be such that he "can no longer show his face."

Seen in these ways, the concern with "face" is not "exaggerated"; it is an integral part of basic Japanese behavior aimed at managing interdependence and maintaining harmonious relations. There is not therefore the "preoccupation" with fears of losing face in Japan that some Americans imagine, since it is usually in everybody's interest to maintain harmony. One is far more likely to lose face in Japan through making mistakes than from any intentional insult by others. Criticism that is thinly veiled in humor, such as sarcasm, is uncommon in Japan. Americans who work closely with Japanese for some time will learn to be cautious in how they treat others, for fear of giving offense.

"Face" is also used in a positive sense in Japan. There is an expression which literally says that a person "has a broad face," meaning the person is well known and has many, useful connections. Someone may even ask the one with the broad face, "May we borrow your face?" where an American in the same situation might say "Can we use your name?" The slight difference in expressions is revealing, the "name" being what is given to the individual person, the "face" being that which is shown to others.

When Americans and Japanese work together problems related to "face" do often arise. The most obvious, but not the most common, occurs when an American embarrasses a Japanese associate in public, either unintentionally or perhaps in the spirit of making a friendly joke. Unfortunately, the American may not sense what has happened or be aware of the degree of discomfort caused or how detrimental it can be to future relations. (When face has been lost in Japan it is much more difficult to re-establish good relations than is usually the case in America.) The unintended slight is given most easily by younger or lower ranking Americans who fail to express appropriate respect to an older or higher ranking Japanese.

Japanese can be as embarrassed when they are singled out for praise as for blame. American managers working in Japan can create problems when they single out, for example, one of several secretaries for praise. Although more subtle, it is an act of giving exceptional attention to one individual, of separating one from the group. Also, as noted elsewhere, failure to include people who expect, as members of the organization, to be included can cause a loss of face.

There is also much effort among Japanese to help "cover" for others, to work together to prevent or to "save" situations that might otherwise prove embarrassing to colleagues or friends. In this regard considerations of "face" may take precedence over other considerations such as meeting a deadline, being consistent, or being frank about what is going on. One important means of avoiding loss of face for others is to pretend not to notice certain things which, if broached directly, could cause embarrassment. Even here, however, cultural differences may complicate the situation. The American may want—or says he wants—frankly stated opinions of his actions. "I need your feedback," he may tell his co-worker; "Please tell me if I offend you or do anything wrong so that I can learn and improve." But the Japanese are likely to be reluctant to give such opinions directly if they feel it would be embarrassing. The American will probably have to learn to read other signals, make his own inferences, and test them out less directly in some appropriate setting with the right person. He might even seek the advice of a cross-cultural consultant or someone knowledgeable about Japanese-American behavioral styles. Conversely, the American may have to temper "constructive criticism" or a "performance evaluation" so as not to cause embarrassment.

A Japanese executive who has worked almost equal amounts of time in Tokyo and in New York said he was amused by the American expression "to be thin skinned," meaning "too sensitive to what others say." "I think Americans who work with Japanese need to become more thin skinned, and Japanese who work with Americans—particularly in New York—need to become more 'thick skinned,' because the meaning and consequences of what others say about us or how others treat us are so different in each country."

One other observation about "face." The *kanji*, the Chinese character, for "face" is the same as the character for "mask." This reminds us that "face" is what we show outwardly and not necessarily an expression of our true feelings, though it may be that too. But as noted in the discussion of *honne* and *tatemae*, the outward expression is just as valued as inner feelings.

4

四

Interaction: Behavior, Reactions, and Interpretations

Mutual Perception of Communication Habits

There are Americans who have lived in Japan for years who amuse themselves by playing a game called "You've been in Japan too long when . . ." The object of the game is simply to name some habit or social phenomenon that has come to seem quite ordinary which, in fact, seemed extraordinary when the American first encountered it in Japan. "You've been in Japan too long when you automatically start bowing into the telephone when a friend calls," or "You've been in Japan too long when you leave the men's room and automatically dry your hands on your handkerchief." Psychologists might well examine the game and those who play it to learn something about identity and acculturation. It might better be said about the players that they have been in Japan just long enough for such actions or reactions to seem natural and not require special thought and attention.

What is curious is that while Americans can be conscious of some mannerisms that seem "very Japanese," at the same time they can be totally ignorant of how their own behavior is perceived. The same is true, of course, of Japanese who work with Americans. It is revealing, therefore, to look at some of the communication habits of Americans that Japanese notice as especially troubling or irksome, and to look at similar behaviors of the Japanese that Americans sometimes complain about.

The following lists were compiled on the basis of surveys and interviews conducted in Japan during the last several years. Certainly not every American is faulted on all of the items on the list, nor do all Americans complain about every Japanese in these terms. But these are communication habits which are mentioned with sufficient frequency to convince us that they constitute areas of significant misunderstanding.

"Those Americans!"

American habits that Japanese grumble about

1. *Americans talk too much.* "they seem uncomfortable with silences and as a result chatter on about meaningless things."

2. *Americans interrupt other people*—even finishing sentences for them. "This can be irritating, especially if we are unsure of our English, and even more so if what the American says is not what we had intended to say at all. We don't want to be misunderstood but also we don't want to have to correct or contradict our American friends."

3. *American don't listen enough.* "They seem too eager to raise questions and put forth their own ideas before hearing

out what is to be said. Perhaps because they are uncomfortable with silences or because they like to talk, they misinterpret quiet but attentive Japanese as shy or weak.'

4. *Americans seem to think that if they don't tell you something you won't know it.* "This is most irritating when they talk on and on about their own abilities and accomplishments. Though they may only be trying to be clear, they often sound like they are boasting. They should have more faith in our understanding of who they are. After all, if we didn't know about them, why would we be talking together in the first place?"

5. *Americans are too direct in asking questions, giving opinions, and poking fun.* "This can put us on the spot and cause awkwardness or feelings of discomfort. Some even mistake our embarrassed laughter as appreciation."

6. *Americans fail to express thanks and appreciation sufficiently.* "Many Americans think that a simple 'thank you' is enough. When meeting a Japanese they haven't seen for a while they forget to acknowledge appreciation for past favors."

7. *Americans are reluctant to admit faults or limitations: they seldom apologize, even just to be polite.* "Even if they are late for a meeting, they are likely to try to justify being late with some excuse. They seem more concerned to explain *their* behavior than to be sensitive to others' feelings."

8. *American managers and directors give more attention to individuals than to the entire group or team.* "It is embarrassing to a person who is singled out, and it can be bad for the morale of the larger group. Americans also often fail to go through proper channels, which can sometimes cause people to lose face and which usually causes confusion."

9. *Americans do not appreciate the importance of certain formalities in Japan.* "We Japanese don't expect Americans to act like Japanese, but it is embarrassing when Americans joke about some of our formalities or matters of social etiquette."

10. *Americans are too time conscious.* "They are always hurrying to meet some deadline, glancing at their watches, or scheduling activities."

"Those Japanese!"

Japanese habits that Americans grumble about

1. *The Japanese are so polite and so cautious that you never know what they are thinking.* "Some Japanese ask probing questions but most just listen quietly, nodding and seeming to agree. It is irritating when you later hear that the Japanese you were talking to had doubts and disagreements but didn't say them at the time."

2. *The Japanese use vague words and ambiguous expressions so that it is hard to know where they stand.* "Sometimes even other Japanese say that they are not sure of what to conclude about some discussions in Japanese."

3. *The Japanese are conformists.* "They seem to be afraid to assert their individual opinions on their own merits. They seem too conscious of what other people might be thinking." "Spontaneous they are not."

4. *The Japanese are forever expressing thanks and appreciation for this or that.* "It is hard to know how much of what they say is sincere and how much is mere ritual."

5. *The Japanese are always apologizing, even when there is nothing to apologize for.* "Sometimes the apology seems thoughtful, but it can seem subservient, especially in mature men."

6. *The Japanese seem to be always weighing the meaning of this or that action and then acting as if everything had to fit into some large Japanese scheme of things.* "They seem unable to accept a token gift or even an invitation to lunch without immediately responding in kind to repay the favor. As a result they seem more sensitive to propriety and form then to real personal feelings."

7. *The Japanese are notoriously slow in making decisions.* "Even after making a decision the reasons why something is to be done or not done and who is responsible may not be at all clear."

8. *Japanese, for all their modesty, can be very ethnocentric.* "They assume that no foreigner can understand things they regard as uniquely Japanese. 'Since you're not Japanese, you can't understand,' they say." "It is hard to have really good Japanese friends. They are too exclusive. They seemed pleased when you express an interest in something Japanese and they may explain things, but I really don't think they expect a *gaijin* to understand."

9. *The Japanese are very imitative, faddish and overly impressed by status.* "The Japanese are the most status conscious people in the world, from schools to whiskeys to corporations."

10. *The Japanese are too formal.* "Japanese men only seem spontaneous when they are out drinking."

Key Issues

Speaking, listening and silence

Most Americans are familiar with the expression "silence is golden," but few know it in its most familiar form in Japan: "Speech is silver, but silence is golden." Indeed, Japanese proverbs indicating distrust of words and the value of silence are numerous. "Hollow drums make the most noise" is a favorite.

Americans tend to believe that if something hasn't been put into words it has not been communicated, and that if someone has something to say, he should say it. Studies show that American children are encouraged to speak more and do, indeed, speak more than do Japanese children of the same age at home and at school. Speaking or "speaking up" indicates for Americans a person who is paying attention, who has ideas or opinions or information. Though everybody knows people who seem to talk too much, the greater concern of Americans is more likely to be that they do not speak up or speak out enough.

Conversely, Americans usually associate silence in social situations with something negative—tension, hostility, awkwardness, or shyness. And, although Americans in some situations clearly associate "speaking" with "authority" ("let me do the talking"), both experience and folklore supply numerous examples of the little man who spoke out and whose words carried the day.

The Japanese attitudes toward speech and silence are quite different. Speaking in itself is not regarded as highly as it is in the West generally. A Japanese is hard put to think of any "great speeches" or even ringing quotations of Japanese speakers.[2] Public speeches tend to be formalistic, with no surprises. Writing, however, holds enormous prestige.

Speaking too much is associated in Japan with immaturity or a kind of empty-headedness. It is also associated with women. There is a Japanese character made up of three *kanji* (Chinese characters) for "woman": the character means "noise."

Silences, on the other hand, have many meanings in a Japanese setting. Silence is not simply the absence of sound or speech, a void to be filled, as Americans tend to regard it. Not speaking can sometimes convey respect for the person who has spoken or the ideas expressed. Silence can be a medium that the parties share, a means of unifying, in contrast to words which separate. Silence in conversations is often

[2] There was a serious disagreement between the Americans and Japanese members of the film crew during the making of the television series, *"Shōgun."* In one scene Toronaga gives a stirring speech to his troops and they all shout his name to show enthusiastic loyalty. Such a scene, which would have made perfect sense in Europe, England or the U.S., seemed totally, culturally, out of place in Japan.

compared to the white space in brush paintings or calligraphy scrolls. A picture is not richer, more accurate, or more complete if such spaces are filled in. To do so would be to confuse and detract from what is presented.

Japanese and Americans often confuse each other in the way they speak and treat silence. An American asks a Japanese a question and there is a pause before the Japanese responds. If the question is fairly direct, the pause may be even longer as the Japanese considers how to avoid a direct answer. The American, however, may assume that the pause is because the question was not clearly understood and hence he may rephrase the question. It often happens that the American is himself just uncomfortable with the silence and is trying to fill in with words to reduce his own uneasiness. In any case, the additional verbalization is only likely to make the situation more difficult for the Japanese. Not only has the American asked two or more questions in the space appropriate for one, he has separated himself by not sharing in a thoughtful silence.

Japan's feudal history has influenced current day attitudes toward speaking and keeping silent. To fit in was to know one's place; to speak out might well mean to lose one's head. Along with so many other features of Japanese society, attitudes toward speaking have changed considerably; older people complain that younger people talk too much these days. Listening respectfully is an appropriate behavior for one in a subordinate position—that is, one who is younger, of lower rank, serving as host, and so on. (If of the same age, rank, etc., women will defer to men; if women are older or of higher rank, men should defer to women.) While this pattern has its counterparts in America, age, seniority, rank, and role as host or guest are not nearly as influential as in Japan. An American supervisor may admire an employee who speaks right up—depending upon what the person has to say. In Japan, it is more likely that the "speaking right up" in itself would be offensive. The American *bright* young man becomes the *brash* young man in Japanese terms.

A top American executive based in Tokyo discovered after working in Japan for several years that he had been misjudging Japanese associates by evaluating them largely on the basis of their styles of listening and speaking. "I just didn't realize that I had been taking quick, clear, direct questions as a sign of an alert listener and a good staff member. I wonder how many Japanese I have misjudged, in and out of the office, simply because they didn't give me that kind of response. Now I wonder if I hired the worst—least typically Japanese—and dismissed some of the best."

Turn taking

Another common American conversational habit is to try to help complete sentences or phrases begun by the other person. Some people do this more than others; research conducted in America shows that higher status people will "help" complete sentences of lower status people rather than the other way around. American men finish sentences for women far more than do women for men, and Americans end sentences for Japanese more than Japanese for Americans. It may be meant primarily to show that one is listening and following along, but the Japanese may interpret it as impatience, aggressiveness, failure to show respect or a simple exercise of power. This is a small but important intercultural communication problem of which most Americans working with Japanese are probably unaware, but it is the kind of problem that can exert considerable strain on the relationship.

The line and the curve: directness and indirectness

American and Japanese conversational styles differ, one might say, geometrically. The American preference is for the linear—lines of argument, lines of reasoning. "The bottom line" has moved from the accountant's ledger to refer to any "base line" principle. These lines move to points—Americans come to the point, make several points when discussing something. Lines and points, like the pattern in the American flag.

In contrast, the Japanese style, like the Japanese flag, favors the curve. To go around something rather than "straight to the point" is preferred. Points stick out. Points might injure someone. In Japan one takes care to avoid either eventuality.

Americans grow up with a whole set of negative expressions about the circular—"going around in circles," "beating around the bush," and the like. A circular style is distinctly unattractive. It suggests vague thinking or a fear of saying what one really means, both of which Americans criticize. It also seems most inefficient. If Americans want to contact someone, it is a virtue to do so directly—the shortest distance between two points is a straight line.

From the Japanese perspective, however, being direct and to the point can mean being insensitive to the other's feelings as well as lacking in aesthetic subtlety, at least in the setting of a formal business meeting. In other settings Japanese can be more direct about some matters than the Americans. Said a Japanese professional interpreter:

> "Americans can be just as indirect as the Japanese, but they are indirect about different things, and being indirect carries a different meaning. Americans are usually indirect when something very sensitive is being discussed or when they are nervous about how the other person might react. Whenever Americans are indirect, I suspect that *something* is going on!
>
> Japanese indirectness is a part of our way of life. It is not because we are such kind and considerate people that we worry so about the other's reactions. It is just that we know that our own fates and fortunes are always bound up with others. I think

you can value directness when you value individualism, or when you are with people you know and trust completely."

What does directness mean to the Japanese?

"It depends on the situation, of course. We're still more direct about some things than Americans who retain some Victorian language habits, even though they might not think so. But generally we associate the American sort of directness with the expression of power or authority within a group, like a general barking out commands. We do that too, maybe even more than Americans, *within our group*—that is, the boss can do that. It's when somebody talks that way to people who are equals or not well known that it is a problem."

Do the two languages, Japanese and English, contribute to the problem?

"It is true that English is more active than Japanese. In interpreting from Japanese to English, I often have to change from the passive to the active voice. Japanese also seems more abstract, more vague—even to other Japanese—than English (or American English) seems. Language is probably part of this, but mostly I think being direct or indirect depends on a person's sense of appropriateness."

Words in and out of context

When the Tokyo branch manager of an American company heard from New York about potentially serious problems that might befall his office, he was careful to tell no one until he had more information. Nevertheless, within days he got the clear impression that others in the office knew something was up and, if anything, were even more worried than he was. He was baffled as to how the report might have leaked out, until a Japanese co-worker had the courage to ask about the problem. The American explained what he had heard and then asked, "But how did everybody here know something was wrong?" "Oh, that was obvious. For the past week you have come to the office with a sad face. That scared us."

Japanese "read" faces and postures and clothing to a much greater extent, and with more accuracy, than do most Americans. Moreover, in many ways Japanese prefer nonverbal messages to those expressed in words. Americans, on the other hand, place much more trust in words than on fleeting impressions. These are not mere quirks of behavior, but rather they arise out of two different value systems. In one, spoken words are not so highly prized and are not necessarily to be taken at face value. In the other, verbal messages are central and people are held accountable for what they say.

Even veteran American managers in Japan report times when some personnel problem suddenly bursts forth, like a volcano exploding. A secretary who seemed so content suddenly announces she is resigning, or frustrations of staff workers spill out into the open. The American reaction is: "What happened? Why didn't you tell me there was a problem?" The Japanese are likely to think, if not say, "We were 'telling you,' but not in words. Why didn't you sense the problem in time?" For Americans, putting thoughts in words is the only way another person can be expected to know what's on someone's mind. Japanese assume there are other and better ways to express some things. As Masao Kunihiro has put it, "For Americans, using words is *the* means of communication. For Japanese it is *a* means."

In his book, *Beyond Culture,* anthropologist Edward Hall develops a theory of communication which is helpful in understanding Japanese and American relations. In Hall's terms we can put our trust in words to understand and be understood, or we can look for meaning in the *context* within which the words are spoken—such as who says the words, where and how they are spoken and so on. Cultures differ in what they emphasize. On a world scale, America ranks very high in its trust in words and very low in its reliance on context.

Japan, and indeed much of the world outside northern Europe, ranks high in the trust placed on context and low in trust on words.

There are several reasons for this difference. One concerns how well people know each other. A husband and wife who have been married for many years can often sense what each other is thinking without having to be told because they have shared so much that just a few words taps a reservoir of meaning. Strangers, of course, can assume little about what the other is thinking and thus have to rely on words. Americans are often strangers to one another. Compare, for example, the homogeneity of Japan to the pluralism of the U.S., the value of the group or interdependence of the Japanese to the importance of individualism for Americans, the lifetime employment of the Japanese to the relatively high job mobility of Americans, and the sheer amount of time Japanese co-workers spend together at the plant or office and after hours to the separation of work and play by Americans.

Context is important in other matters as well—contracts, for example. In cultures where context gives meaning, a contract represents a kind of best guess, a formalized point in a changing reality so that if the terms of a contract cannot be met, the parties should get together and discuss things again. Where words outweigh context, then the terms of a contract tend to be fixed and rigid. This is exactly the situation with regard to Japanese and American views of contracts and they fall precisely in these two positions. In a survey in Japan, people were asked what should be done if a contract has been signed but after a period of time it was impossible to fulfill the terms because conditions had changed. Less than a quarter of those surveyed responded that "a contract is a contract," and people should feel bound by its terms. Two-thirds chose the alternative—to talk it out with the other party and see what adjustments might be made.

Japanese sometimes describe Americans as not simply precise and direct but also "legalistic," at least when a formal commitment is called for. As noted, Americans may describe the Japanese in such a case as vague or abstract. If it happens that a Japanese wishes to renegotiate a contract due to changed conditions, the Americans (or Australians or Germans) may become angry and refuse to budge. There have been some dramatic instances of just this kind in recent years.

Similarly, when a Japanese is hired by a Japanese company he or she might not be given a precise job description; the new employee may not even know what the salary will be, a condition that few Americans would feel comfortable with. "How do you know you will even get paid?" an American asked a Japanese friend who described this situation. The American wants the promise stated clearly in words. The Japanese places the trust more in other matters—the company's reputation, the person who may have recommended the candidate, and so on.

Erabi and *awase*

"*Erabi* and *awase*" is not the name of a Japanese law firm. Rather they are terms which an astute Japanese social scientist, Kin Hide Mushakoji, has used to distinguish divergent negotiating styles of Americans and Japanese.

The *erabi* style is that of a choice-maker, one who chooses or selects—the style associated with American negotiators. On the assumption that one has some control over events and that one enters into a bargaining situation only when one's goal is clear, the *erabi* style is marked by a series of choices which lead directly to the desired goal. In presenting his theory, Mushakoji notes that these choices are of an "either/or," "yes or no" sort; he compares them with the sort of choices one makes in playing chess. Americans who speak about their "game plan" clearly describe the *erabi* way of thinking.

The *awase* style, on the other hand, is characterized by continuous adjustment to an ever changing environment. "*Awase*" comes from "*awaseru*," meaning to adjust to something else or to combine; this is the style associated with the Japanese. From an *awase* point of view one cannot proceed toward a fixed goal but rather must adjust to changing and uncertain conditions. The *awase* style negotiator, therefore, may not have a fixed goal in mind until after entering into negotiations and sensing what might be possible under the circumstances. Consistent with this, the language of *awase* style is "more-or-less" rather than "either-or." Nuance and shades of meaning are very important.

A television set provides an analogy for the two kinds of negotiating styles. The *erabi* or American style is likened to the knob which selects the channel. One must choose either one channel or another. The *awase* style is more like the volume control which may be adjusted to be slightly softer or a little louder, depending on circumstances. This, then, is comparable to the Japanese style of negotiating.

What happens when Japanese and Americans attempt to negotiate and the *awase* and *erabi* styles meet? In the first place there may be a clash of protocols. The Americans may want to put forth their proposals immediately, to "lay their cards out on the table"—again the game metaphor is revealing. The Japanese may not be prepared to do so; they may want to spend much more time during which, in effect, they can come to know the Americans better so as to see what might be worked out. Thus the one side may be viewed as too "fast," too blunt or aggressive, and possibly too uncompromising. The other side, in contrast, may be perceived as too "slow" and too cautious, too guarded about their position.

The *awase* style negotiator also *assumes* that the adjustments will be reciprocal, though the expectation of a *quid pro quo* may not be stated. Americans do not make this same assumption. There are many cases in business and government relations where the Japanese have been startled to find that Americans did not reciprocate as expected.

The *awase* (Japanese) mode of thinking also expects there to be an unavoidable gap between form and reality. "We say things should be this way but we know that in practice it is not so simple." This is very different from the *erabi* style which *usually* is most concerned about the formal outcome of negotiations—the agreement or contract or whatever. Americans want to have detailed and binding contracts in many instances where the Japanese would prefer a less precise document which serves as a symbol of their efforts to work together. As a result, Japanese may continue to negotiate for favors after a contract has been signed, a position which Americans or others accustomed to the *erabi* mode regard as most improper.

Your most enchanted listener

Years ago the semanticist Wendell Johnson wrote a delightful book called *Your Most Enchanted Listener*. What Johnson had in mind was that we are our most enchanted listeners when we talk. The title came to mind when visiting with a Japanese friend who studied in the States and who has been living for a number of years in Honolulu. "There is one habit of Americans I still have not gotten used to," she said, "and it bothers me most when I come back here from being in Japan. The difference is so obvious: Japanese talk about each other, and Americans love to talk about themselves."

She explained, "If I tell a Japanese friend that I was just in Los Angeles, my friend will ask me what I saw, how I liked it, and so on. But if I tell an American the same thing, he will say, 'Oh, Los Angeles? I've got a cousin who lives in Long

Beach. I've never been there. I really like L.A., and when I went shopping there last year . . .' It's really irritating the way Americans feel they can just turn the conversation to talk about themselves if they want to."

This sort of exchange does not always happen, but it seems far more common, and acceptable, among Americans than among Japanese. The Japanese consciousness of the other person—the interdependent concern—stands in sharp contrast to the more independent or individualistic American focus. Not surprisingly this is reflected in the communication styles of the two peoples and in their evaluations of each other.

The difference in orientations is apparent when friends who have not seen each other for a while happen to meet. Americans are likely to ask about each other and tell each other about where they have been or what they have been doing. Who speaks first does not seem to matter very much. When Japanese friends meet, one is likely to begin by thanking the other for some previous favor or gift or letter that was sent. Most often, a reference to the last time they were together is part of this greeting. Thus they re-establish a particular continuing relationship.

Americans in Japan are well advised to follow the Japanese pattern described above. It is an easy rule for Americans to follow since so often they are in some social debt to Japanese for favors given (often translating or interpreting or other assistance). To do so begins the conversation in a familiar and thus comfortable manner while at the same time communicating thoughtfulness and sincere appreciation. To fail to do so suggests a lack of concern for the other, or thoughtlessness.

Americans sometimes misinterpret the Japanese custom of expressing thanks or inquiring about some past event as "overdoing it." It also may embarrass Americans for, as one said, "the Japanese always find something to thank me for before I can come up with something to thank them for. I sometimes think it's a kind of one-upsmanship." The interpretation of thanking as a kind of game is actually not very helpful here. The desire to begin by referring to something that relates the parties, as mentioned, is one factor. Another reason is the genuine uneasiness Japanese occasionally feel about being in social debt; better to err on the side of excessive politeness than to be insufficiently polite. (Ill-mannered behavior, remember, reflects poorly not only on the individual but on the family, school or company of which the person is a part.) A third reason is that this *is* the proper form, and doing what is expected is very important.

Humility and politeness

Modesty is a virtue, a social grace, in both societies. A boastful, self-centered person is as tedious in Seattle as in Sapporo. Japanese and Americans alike appreciate a hero who brushes off words of praise for his actions. There are, however, some differences.

As a rule, Americans can risk sounding "overly modest" by American standards and still be well within the realm of "appropriately modest" by Japanese standards. A more important rule for Americans, though, is to resist speaking about oneself or one's achievements in ways that are self-promoting. While there is something in American culture that allows or even encourages a person to "sell yourself," the notion of merchandising oneself does not set well with the Japanese. Remember, in Japan one does not like to stand out or be singled out, even by others; it is far worse to promote oneself.

Describing the difference in terms of Eastern and Western values generally, a Chinese journalist in Japan recalled the heroes in the martial arts movies, like the Kung Fu films. "You'll notice that Bruce Lee never shows how good he is until he has to act. Only the bad guys and the unskilled show off. That's not just part of the Bruce Lee character, that's an Asian virtue." Among the proverbs one hears quoted the most when Japanese talk about Japanese values (particularly in contrast to Western values) is: "The clever hawk hides its claws."

The expression of modesty is apparent in a variety of situations. There are Japanese "personals" in the classified ads in some publications that are similar to those that appear in big cities in the States, but where an American ad might begin, "Attractive, athletic, male with a good sense of humor seeks . . .," the comparable Japanese ad might read, "Though I am not very good looking . . ."

When one offers something to another person, such as a gift or a meal that one has prepared, the same kind of depreciation is called for in Japan. There are set expressions for such humility: "It's nothing," or, "It's nothing special." Never take such apologies at face value. The hostess who apologizes to her guests that "there is nothing (special) to offer you" has probably spent the better part of two days planning and preparing the meal. Of course the guest should protest such disclaimers.

What is true of speaking about oneself or something one offers another person is also true of speaking about one's family. Because each person identifies so closely with one's family, to praise one's own spouse or children is a little like praising oneself. Japanese mothers, who are likely to be friends because their children are friends, will say how wonderful the other's son or daughter is, when in fact the mother's own son or daughter may be the brightest kid in the class.

There is a set expression in Japanese which means "my foolish wife," and which is used by men who in fact are very proud of their wives. The reluctance to advertise the good qualities of one's immediate family is one reason Japanese find it strange when American businessmen keep pictures of their wives or families on their desks at the office. "Is it because you miss your family so much that you keep their picture on your desk?" one Japanese asked an American. "No," said the American, "I guess it just helps to remind me why I'm here working." "Oh," said the Japanese, "then that's another difference between us."

See-saw relations

In some ways interpersonal relations in Japan can be likened to what happens on a see-saw. When a person moves in such a way as to cause the other to be elevated, his end tips down to the ground. Was it the lowering that caused the other to rise, or allowing the other to rise that caused oneself to be lowered? Or is it that these are both part of the same process? Japanese show respect and express gratitude and politeness by elevating, in words and actions, the other person. Like the logic of the see-saw, they can do the same by humbling themselves. Both the deference which raises the other and the humility which humbles oneself are basic principles of interpersonal relations in Japan. Indeed, the logic of the see-saw is sometimes almost comic when two persons attempt to out-humble themselves or out-compliment the other.

Americans may do as well as the Japanese in extolling praise for or expressing concern about the other, but their culture has not prepared them to be quite as self-effacing as the Japanese can be. Perhaps Americans lack the kind of set expressions in the language that make it easy. More likely, though, they are encouraged to be assertive. Some Japanese believe that Americans feel they have to advertise their abilities or nobody will know about them; if so, they may also worry that their expressions of modesty might be taken too seriously.

Because of the implicit hierarchy in Japanese relations, where one is always conscious of who defers to whom, there is little ambiguity about the meaning of polite amenities in Japan. So often they simply reaffirm a relationship, treating a person as he or she expects or feels entitled to be treated. When this is lacking, the person may be irritated or confused. The same thing sometimes happens in the U.S., of course. When customers feel they are not being treated courteously by salespeople in a store, or when parents feel they are not shown some modicum of respect from their offspring, they are bothered or feel hurt. In the army that sort of thing is called insubordination. American culture, however, discourages people from expecting any special treatment that has not been "earned." The expectation of being treated in a certain way by virtue of one's relationship with another is the norm in Japan. One does not expect to have to negotiate each new relationship. Thus it is that Japanese managers in factories can dress like everybody else and eat in the company cafeteria alongside the workers without feeling that their position is threatened: everybody knows the relationship without its having to be demonstrated outwardly.

Just as there is hierarchy in human relations which guide communication, there are also hierarchies in settings. In a traditional Japanese room, for example, there is a "low place," (*shimoza*) and a "high place" (*kamiza*); the former being a place to sit nearest the door, the latter being away from the door with one's back to the *tokonoma* (where a flower arrangement or calligraphy hanging may be displayed). The person who serves tea or who goes in and out of the door to bring files or copies of reports to persons gathered at a meeting will sit in the low place. The person who is the guest of honor or the eldest in the family or the highest ranking person in the organization will sit in the high place. The only time there may be some dispute about who sits where is when a guest is politely declining the honor of sitting at the *kamiza,* an honor he or she will eventually accept. It is the see-saw principle at work again.

While who sits where and who defers to whom will be perfectly clear within an organization where people know each other, what happens when strangers meet? How does one know how to act appropriately? Several points should be noted.

First of all, Japanese do not always know how to tip that see-saw when they first meet someone, particularly if the meeting is informal and unexpected, and if there is no clear difference in age. They may ask some of the same questions Americans would in the same situation, but do so more cautiously and with an ear to learning at least who is older. In business and professional circles, *meishi* (business cards) will be exchanged, and the recipients will pay most attention to the other's position in the company. Companies or other organizations, of course, also have their own status and relative rank, just as they do anywhere, and this too enters into the calculation.

Japanese are also more likely than Americans to do their homework in preparing for meetings with others. The Japanese will want to know at least enough about the person he is meeting for the first time in order to act appropriately, rather than trying to figure out the relationship at the time of the meeting. All this has to do with more than just *aisatsu* (greetings), of course, for it also anticipates what kind of future relationship, if any, should be encouraged. This desire to be prepared for meetings is one reason Japanese prefer to use an intermediary in making introductions, for the third party can help to clarify a situation in a way that avoids awkwardness and potential embarrassment. It is also a reason that Japanese are uncomfortable with "cold calls" from persons who want to do business. American businesspeople who arrive at a Japanese company without warning do not make a good impression and are not likely to be well received. The company is literally unprepared to receive them.

Time and time again

The theme of time comes up over and over when Japanese and Americans describe difficulties in working together. There is good reason to believe that attitudes toward time are significant in intercultural relations everywhere in the world, but the American and Japanese case has some special features. Outwardly the two countries seem to share a number of important characteristics. Both value promptness, both utilize speedy technologies, and in their major commercial centers, New York and Tokyo, both seem to be equally fast paced. Some Americans who have worked in Tokyo for a number of years and then return to New York even complain that things move too slowly in Manhattan!

A more common American complaint is that it seems to take a long time to get anything done in Japan. Decisions seem to take forever. The truism, however, is that Japanese decisions are slow but once the decision is made, implementation is very fast—since everyone was in on the decision. For Americans, the opposite: fast decisions, slow implementation. For the same reasons, Americans are seen by Japanese as too driven by deadlines.

On the other hand, Americans who are supposed to be "future oriented" are seen by Japanese to be lacking in foresight and long range planning. And the Japanese, whose society is far more conservative and known to revere the past, are pressing ahead with innovative technologies that are speeding up changes in societies all over the world. What is going on here?

Broadly speaking, the consciousness of past, present, and future differs sharply between the Japanese and the Americans. The past plays an important role in making decisions and guiding actions in Japan. Age means experience and wisdom. Thus, just as a younger person defers to one who is older, older organizations command respect, too. One problem Americans face in entering into relations with Japanese enterprises is that the American companies may not have been in Japan long enough to inspire the needed trust and confidence. The past is a clue to the future, after all, and if a company has been around for only ten or twenty years, how can one be sure that it will still be around twenty years from now? Such is the thinking of the Japanese.

Moreover, Americans simply are not encouraged by their culture to have the kind of reverence for age that Japanese culture instills, whether it is a matter of respect for elders or for old buildings or old plants (like very old *bonsai*) or carp that live longer than people. American culture looks more to innovation, change, energy—qualities associated with younger people and appropriate to a younger nation.

American attention is directed toward the near future—one, two, perhaps five years from now. Because Americans expect and value change, including their own mobility, and feel most comfortable when grounded in facts and figures, they tend not to look very far ahead. Americans are not given to very long-range planning. Americans are perceived, whether accurately or not, as being concerned with matters as they arise, of anticipating only what is just ahead. Many Japanese who have worked in American companies, however, see this concern as an excessive preoccupation with deadlines and schedules. The Japanese treatment of deadlines is more flexible, a goal to aim for but not binding if circumstances make meeting it difficult. (More on this in the next chapter.)

The vagueness of Japanese speech, from the American point of view, or the overly direct and precise use of language by the Americans, from the Japanese point of view, also emerges when time is an issue. A proposal may be made by an American team, and the Japanese may respond, "We will study the matter." That is too vague for many Americans who will press for something more specific: "How soon can you get back to us? In one or two weeks? In a month?" But that, in turn, makes the Japanese uneasy.

An advisor who has worked in Japanese and American relations for more than forty years said of the above situation that the problem is not so much concerned with time as with the psychological interpretation of time. "Americans and Japanese have a different idea of what is a 'reasonable amount of time' partly because their organizations operate so differently. Many more people in the typical Japanese organization will have to consider the matter than would be true of an American company. That's part of it. But the Japanese hate to be pressed to act prematurely. The pressure can create tremendous anxiety when there should be no need to set a specific deadline." He added, "Americans, though, feel anxious if they don't have that specific deadline."

Americans and Japanese also mentally divide time differently. Americans are concerned about having an equitable balance between "work time" and "private time," which may mean mostly time with one's family. While this sort of distinction is understandable to the Japanese, the distinction between "formal" work and "informal" times for socializing is more relevant to them.

What often happens is this: an American in Japan, having worked eight hours and possibly "overtime" as well, is ready to go home, or at least leave the office and co-workers. To feel obliged to continue working or to go out to socialize with business associates or staff seems an intrusion upon his own private time. His Japanese counterpart, on the other hand, welcomes the chance to shift from the formal setting of the office to the informal setting of a restaurant or bar where he can get to know the others better or just enjoy their company in a relaxed setting. In the process he will also learn a bit of useful gossip related to the business and he may be able to say things that could not be said in the office. (See the later section, After Hours.)

Some Americans do not understand the importance of the "informal time." Most who work with Japanese for any period of time, however, are aware of the importance of the informal setting, but still may feel resentment that they have to "give up their own time" to go drinking with the people from the office. Obviously they may feel even more frustrated if there are counter-pressures from their families to come home.

The opposite situation occurs for Japanese who work for American companies in New York or elsewhere. They feel frustrated and left out when all of their American colleagues leave work and head for home. They feel there is no chance to really get to know these people or to become friends or to hear and say some things that don't get said at the office.

5

五

Managerial Styles, Japanese and American

Beyond Comparison

A Manhattan book dealer said he had never seen anything like the surge of interest American readers have recently shown for books on Japanese management. With books like Ezra Vogel's *Japan as Number One* and William Ouchi's *Theory Z* leading the best seller charts, there have been a spate of other books, articles, television features, and seminars telling Americans how Japan does it. Many have argued that Americans have much to learn from the Japanese, while others have raised doubts about transferring methods from one culture to another. In this writer's opinion, the most remarkable fact about the Japan boom in the U.S. is that for the first time Americans have considered the possibility of learning from another culture in areas where Americans had thought they excelled. In that regard Japan deserves special credit, for this might lead to a greater openness and curiosity and learning across other cultural boundaries that rarely occur in the U.S.

Left out of much of this public discussion of comparative management is any guidance on how American managers might best work with Japanese staff, or, as is increasingly likely to be an issue, how American staff can best work with Japanese management. The chart on pages 64 through 66 brings together many of the themes already presented and adds to them some matters of particular interest to managers, such as promotions.

Still it is necessary to go beyond comparisons. What kind of advice do successful American managers in Japan give newcomers? During months of interviewing dozens of American and Japanese managers in Japan, several issues and ways of relating to Japanese staff appeared. Here are some.

Don't Just Do Something, Stand There

Asked what advice he would give incoming American managers, a top executive who has worked in Tokyo fifteen years said, "I'd tell him not to do anything for the first six months." Was this serious advice? "Well, it's worth a try. I've seen a lot more problems caused by Americans trying to do things too quickly than waiting too long to act."

Many Japanese have remarked on what they see as an American tendency to want to act rather than seem to be doing nothing. Said one, "Americans have a 'seize the moment for this chance may never come again' mentality. We Japanese would rather take enough time to be sure before acting. If we miss some opportunities along the way, we know there will be others." He added that when Americans try to urge Japanese to act quickly to take advantage of some situation, the reaction is almost always negative.

Japanese employees put great trust in the guidance a manager gives. Qualities of consistency and predictability are extremely important; inconsistency, sudden change in plans, and uncertainty are among the worst characteristics of which a manager can be accused. A Japanese told of an American manager who assigned some of his best people to do the necessary preparation to market a new product coming out from the home office. The team worked tirelessly for weeks, only to have the manager announce that New York had cancelled the plan. The staff was demoralized. They also wondered how much authority their boss really had. What would the Japanese manager have done? "If I had any doubts at all, I would have had an outside research team undertake the project," he said. "The impact of anything on your people's morale has to be a main consideration."

No Place Like Home Office

American managers in Japan sometimes act too soon in response to pressures from the home office. However difficult relations might sometimes be between American and Japanese co-workers in Japan, the communication problems between the Americans in the branch office and those in the home office can be just as serious.

> "Those people back home just don't understand the situation here, but I can't explain this culture over the telex. How can I explain about an expenditure of a money gift at a funeral when they're at the level of announcing that our only allowed holidays are the Fourth of July, Thanksgiving and Christmas!"

One person tells of poor Harry—and, he says, there have been hundreds of poor Harrys over the years:

> "The American manager gets here and has almost no overlap time with the guy he's replacing. Everything is new and different and it takes him maybe a year or more to catch on to what it's

Communication and Management Styles

Theme	U.S. pattern	Japanese pattern
Basis of personal identification	primarily as an individual, and then as part of a larger group	always as part of some larger group (family, school, work, nation)
Nature of inter-personal relations	independent individuals who work together based on explicit mutual agreement	interdependent relations among people who work within a context of unstated mutual expectations and obligations
	differences in age, sex, role, and rank should not be emphasized outwardly	differences in age, sex, role, rank, etc., are outwardly acknowledged in interpersonal relations—such as deference shown in speech
Valued qualities in work relations	talent, experience; specialists are sought	ability to get along with others, to evoke and respond to trust; the generalist is cultivated
Promotion and mobility in work relations	based on merit; relatively high upward mobility; relatively less horizontal mobility	based on seniority and merit; relatively low upward mobility and more horizontal movement; life-long employment
Preferred interpersonal communication channels	directness with persons of comparable status; indirect with subordinates	intermediaries essential prior to direct contact; direct and frequent contact between superiors and subordinates
Communication style	explicit, verbal presentation of information, requests, instruction, etc.	implicit, nonverbal (through observation of others and of the situation) and some verbal presentation
	vagueness and ambiguity in communication irritating	vagueness and ambiguity may be positive in giving latitude in interpreting situation and in avoiding conflicts

	emphasis is on expressive forms—speaking and to a lesser extent writing; speech style associated with leadership qualities	emphasis is on perception, receptiveness, observation skills; listening and reading and writing skills valued over public speaking ability
	meaning always close to surface of words "Say what you mean, and mean what you say"	meanings often reside in the situation or context, or are to be read "between the lines" or in what is *not* said
Decision-making	top down; relatively fast; where necessary, decision by vote; consensus, though desirable, is not expected and not sought.	upward (from middle or bottom of organization), relatively slow; consensus through lengthy discussions, informal as well as formal, is expected and sought.
Conflict and confrontation	regarded as inevitable though not necessarily desirable; problems should be dealt with directly and frankly	conflicts and confrontations are to be avoided if at all possible; harmony in interpersonal relations a primary goal; conflicts may be dealt with indirectly through an intermediary, or informally in "after hours" socializing
	conflict management important to deal with issues as they arise	agreement management is important, to prevent problems from occurring; good manager is aware of problem before it is openly presented
Social interaction	some degree of spontaneity, novelty is desired; repartee, "one-upmanship," may be enjoyed.	predictability and ritualized interaction valued until very clear friendships or working

(Continued next page)

(Con't)

	Disagreements can be basis for desired social conversation and stimulation	relations are established. Repartee, sarcasm, "one-upmanship" can be embarrassing or threatening; disagreements in public or social settings (parties) can cause discomfort and embarrassment
Family and work loyalties	immediate family (spouse, children) relations may take precedence over work relations if in conflict; loyalty to task, issue, or professional ability may take precedence over loyalty to organization, if in conflict	loyalty to organization is very strong and may take precedence over immediate family desires (e.g., company outing vs. family vacation); loyalties to parents, benefactors, past teachers, etc., strong; school ties strong and viable; task orientation is subordinate to organizational goals, if in conflict.
Time orientation	present and immediate future (within months or a few years); past serves as reference point for subsequent change or for nostalgia rather than as guide to action; future serves as an attraction but too uncertain for basis of much planning	past, present, and future, all viable, due to deference to age (age of organizations as well as people), interdependence, and lifetime employment. Manager is responsible for stewardship of ongoing institution.

like to work here. So eventually he stops reacting to every request from the home office and begins to advise them on what is appropriate for this culture. Then do you know what happens? The home office thinks, 'We'd better bring him back. Poor Harry's gone native!'"

How one clues in people at the home office to provide the kind of support that allows him to make decisions based on Japanese realities instead of monolithic company policy is a major intercultural problem.

When Company Comes

When higher-ups arrive from New York or Los Angeles for a visit, it can be helpful to give them some advice on how to make the best impression on the Japanese staff. They may have to be warned not to make jokes—which are too often impossible to translate and only confuse people—or not to ask staff members, "What shall I call you? What's your first name?"[3]

For the Japanese staff, the visitors from the home office represent the company and therefore should be introduced around with appropriate respect. Managers who fail to introduce home office visitors weaken morale by seeming to exclude employees. The matter of inclusion is among the most important concerns in any Japanese organization.

All Japanese Secretaries Go Straight to Heaven, They Take So Much Abuse

So said one American executive who has been working in Japan for more than twenty years. He was pointing out that

[3] Except to very close friends, Japanese do not use given names as a form of address, and certainly not with an important visitor. What is worse, some American visitors will not take the trouble to learn Japanese names and insist on bestowing American names on employees! "Oh, I can't pronounce that, I'll just call you 'Pete.' O.K., Pete?" Believe it or not, this sort of thing still happens.

a secretary to an American in Japan often must do many more things than her American counterpart would be asked to do. In addition to the usual range of secretarial duties, they are likely to serve as an occasional translator, interpreter, maker of appointments and arrangements for the boss's domestic situation, shopper for gifts, advisor on customs, and go-between explaining to others what the boss probably meant.

Selecting a good secretary is obviously important. The qualities that Americans look for in staff members are not always the same as what Japanese look for. Americans are likely to put more emphasis on skills, such as typing or using the telex, and be attracted by the person's ability in English, particularly if the candidate has a very American manner. Japanese will be more concerned about how the person will get along with others in the office and appear to Japanese visitors. Therefore, in hiring a secretary—or any employee, for that matter—the advice of other Japanese is important.

It is sometimes said that Japanese who work for American companies are somewhat different from those who work for Japanese companies. In the case of secretaries to American executives, it often happens that when the boss leaves, usually rotated home, the secretary leaves as well. "If I'm going to change bosses, I might as well change companies, too," is the reasoning. This kind of changing rarely happens in Japanese organizations.

What If

If Americans sometimes appear to act too hastily, Japanese are seen by Americans as being cautious to a fault. "They wait until they are almost certain before giving an opinion. Even then they are likely to be more conservative than would most Americans working on the same data. In Japan it is simply not good to be found 'wrong.'"

Americans, on the other hand, are said by Japanese to be

overly attracted by what *might* be possible. "Americans are always asking 'What if this, what if that . . .?' or 'What are the odds of such and such happening?' They ask for estimates about unlikely events and want them given in percentages. Japanese don't think that way, so it's difficult to reply."

Looking Good

Personal appearance is important in what a person communicates. This is as true in Omaha as Osaka. In Japan, however, one's clothing and overall neatness have a special importance. One reason relates to the group identification. If a person is not dressed neatly and appropriately, it reflects poorly upon others. Wives are blamed if their husbands are not as neat as they are expected to be. A company is judged, at least in part, on the appearance of its representatives. Employees are disturbed if their superiors do not make an appropriate appearance.

Dress in Japan is more conservative than in the U.S. Flashy ties or checked sports coats and the more extreme women's styles have no place in Japan. There is also a much stronger sense of what is appropriately worn in specific situations. Casual clothes are generally inappropriate in an office setting, except perhaps when one is working overtime on Saturday. Casual clothes are for casual settings; "serious clothes" for serious settings. As noted, one takes care not to stand out in Japan, and appearing to be out of place is sure to call attention to oneself.

Japanese businessmen, on the average, spend more money for clothes than do their American counterparts. In addition to designer clothes in the large department stores, Japan has a great many local tailors, far more than can be found in American cities. That so many continue to serve the public attests to the importance given to clothing.

The Japanese also have a strong sense of matching colors

of clothing to the season and to the age of persons wearing them. The same notion exists in the U.S., but the lines are more sharply drawn in Japan. Using the color red in clothing, for example, is fine for children and for young women up to the age of twenty or so, but not for men or older women. The reasons arise from Japanese aesthetics, such as associating "bright colors" with youth and more somber tones with age, and not from any color taboos.

The Japanese are far more concerned with aesthetics, design and appearance than are Americans. What is most important is the total "fit" of things, from wearing clothes appropriate to the setting to arranging food. In a Japanese meal, quantity of food counts for little compared to the overall appearance of the meal and how each dish complements the others. Not only are foods arranged attractively; even the dishes on which the foods are served are chosen to match the food and the season. The same is true of flower arrangements and other ornamentation.

Hearts and Minds

"I read a little about Japan before coming here," said a Canadian manager. "I read about the vertical society that sounded almost medieval and I read about how formal and polite the Japanese were, and all that. So I figured I would have to keep at a distance, be very formal and proper, and have no chance to get to know any Japanese as people. I was dead wrong. I soon learned that being cold and aloof was not what the Japanese wanted at all. It wasn't easy at first, but now I think I'm closer to my people here than I was with my people in Toronto."

Japanese say, over and over, that the qualities in a supervisor that they most value are the human qualities of trust, warmth, and a feeling that the person has their best interests at heart. When that is communicated, employees will be extremely loyal and put forth their best efforts. A banker said, "The American coming here should realize that he has much more loyalty here than he may be accustomed to. There's a lot that can be done when you know you have that loyalty."

The good manager may demand hard work from his staff, but he allows the employee some latitude in how things are carried out. "The worst thing a supervisor can do here," said one Japanese consultant, "is to seem to be watching people too closely. It gives us the idea that we are not trusted. Without trust, we cannot keep our faces."

The personal style takes many forms. One manager said he thought it was very important that the manager be the one to hand out the bonus envelopes to each person individually. Many American supervisors make it a point to show genuine interest in the families of their employees, and to attend any major ceremonies to which they are invited, such as weddings or funerals. Being personally interested in the employee's general well-being can be communicated without becoming either "chummy" or paternalistic.

A Japanese manager grows into the role through a long apprenticeship. Those personal qualities are cultivated and recognized before he is selected. American managers in Japan do not have that same advantage. Nevertheless, the American makes a mistake if he strictly follows what his culture encourages: "Don't let personal feelings get in the way." The American is more likely to be concerned with adhering to certain principles, of being fair and treating people like equals. In speaking of these values, one Japanese said, "Those are fine qualities, but they are qualities of the head. We Japanese react from the heart or the *hara*, the gut." Japanese describe themselves as 'emotional people" and many view Americans as excessively "rational," by being logical, analytical and following abstract principles at the expense of personal feelings.

About the worst thing that can happen to a Japanese is to be excluded from his group. Historically, the most severe punishment short of death was to be exiled from one's village. Whereas an American mother who is angry at her child might tell him that he is "grounded" and that he cannot leave the house for a number of hours or days, the Japanese threat is to send the child out and not allow him into the house for a period of time. In the same way, one must watch for a managerial style that excludes employees, whether this takes the form of singling out some people for credit at the expense of others or by-passing people in the decision-making process.

The American manager himself must not be excluded or exclusive. Important information may come his way only during informal gatherings, such as over drinks with staff members. If he rarely joins his staff, he will seem aloof and will miss out on opportunities to know the employees more personally. He will also miss the opportunity to show some of his personal qualities and concerns.

After Hours

Just as Americans divide "work time" from "private time," they also tend to divide "work friends" from other personal friends. The idea of leaving work only to spend still more time socializing with those same people is appalling to many Americans. The Japanese time division, though, is more along the lines of formal and informal. To be sure, private or family time is important for the Japanese, but it is not a primary concern on working days. What happens, then, "after hours" that cannot happen during the work day?

Because the setting is away from the office and, typically, in a restaurant with beer or sake, the mood becomes relaxed, the formality is dropped. It is as inappropriate to be formal in the restaurant as it is to be too casual in the office. Japanese make the switch from one kind of time and place to another very clearly. Americans tend to blur the two, sometimes not being quite formal or serious enough in one setting and not quite silly enough in the other.

In the informal setting, the sense of the group as a whole is maintained, however. As one Japanese put it, "We may play some different tunes, but we're still the same orchestra." This is not a setting where private interests can be pursued while ignoring the rest of the party.

In this informal setting, news is spread and gossip is pursued and joking occurs. An employee who is dissatisfied with something the manager has done might say so here over a few drinks. The *sake-no-ue* (over sake) setting allows for the airing of many feelings that find no appropriate forum in the formal setting of the office. Even better, the next day the person who spoke his mind may go up to the manager and apologize: "Please excuse me for anything I might have said last night. I probably had a few too many drinks." The manager assures him that there is nothing to apologize for and that he looks forward to drinking with him again. But the message has been communicated clearly.

The informal, after hours setting is also regarded by Japanese as the best place to learn about potential business partners. Details of business are not the subject of conversation, for the intent is to learn about each other's personality and character. Until there is confidence about that, no details can be considered. First things first!

The American unfamiliar with this custom may inadvertently block communication just when it is beginning. This is what often happens: after some discussion about business at the office, the Japanese may suggest that the two go have a few drinks and dinner together. The American is likely to see this not as the next step in the development of a working relationship, but as simply a courtesy toward a visitor. He may also feel his private time is being taken up. If he goes but makes it clear he cannot stay very long, or if he declines the invitation outright, he will only make it more difficult for the Japanese to decide about the business matters.

Americans often misconstrue the purposes of the after-hours gatherings. "They are testing me to see how much I can drink," or "They are trying to impress me," or "They want to use up their expense account." Such interpretations miss the point completely and are based on assumptions that come out of a different culture.

6

六

Questions Americans Ask About Japan

Some of the same questions are asked over and over by Americans who become interested in Japan and things Japanese. Here are some of the most frequently asked questions (tourism queries excepted) and some brief answers:

Hasn't Japan become very "Americanized" in recent years?

It was about 125 years ago that Japan opened up to the outside world after a long period of seclusion. From that period (the Meiji era) Japanese delegations traveled everywhere, learning Western forms of every kind of institution, from schooling to transportation to sports. Baseball has been played in Japan for more than a century, for example. So while it is true that there has been a tremendous Western influence exerted in recent years, even as there has been something of a Japanization in the United States, it is not something new. Moreover Americans are likely to think that such changes are continuous and cumulative, so that every day Japan is somehow less Japanese and more Western, but this has not been the case in the past and is not likely to be so in the future.

In recent years, for example, there has been a slight decline in the interest in studying English and an increased interest in a better understanding of the Japanese language. Given the Japanese ability to borrow what is attractive in things foreign and modify them for Japanese use, while rejecting what is not desired, there is no reason to expect Japan to become like a "Western" nation.

Americans also confuse "American" with relative affluence and a high use of technology; Japan today shares those qualities, but that does not make the culture any less Japanese.

Do most people in Japan speak English?

The study of English is required in schools, but in the past and even today, a foreign language is studied mostly for the purpose of reading and, to a lesser extent, writing. Speaking a foreign language has not been so important. This is because the chances of being able to speak with a foreigner were remote in the past— that has changed, obviously—but also because in Japan what is written has always been valued in a way that speaking has not.

High school and some college age students are often eager to practice English and will be bold enough to ask visiting *gaijin* ("foreigners," but actually "foreigners from the West") if they can practice English. It is true that more and more Japanese are traveling, studying, or working abroad, and this has increased the number of people who converse in English. Nevertheless, English is still primarily the compulsory school language which most Japanese regard pretty much as American students have regarded the study of a foreign language at school. (How's your French?)

Visitors who need to ask a stranger for some information—about a train or bus, for example—do best to look for someone who looks like a student for assistance.

What about Chinese? Isn't that like Japanese?

Japanese and Chinese are totally different languages, as different from each other as Chinese is from English. (Japanese, in fact, is distantly related to such far removed languages as Turkish, Hungarian and Finnish.)

Probably the main reason foreigners confuse the two is that the Japanese borrowed the Chinese writing system about a thousand years ago. These are ideographic characters or "picture words" called *"kanji."* Over the years, the characters have changed in both lands, though many characters are still mutually recognizable.

From some of these characters the Japanese also developed two other writing systems, *hiragana* and *katakana,* which represent sounds, rather than being "images," and are used for writing prepositions, verb endings, all borrowed words, and so on. These phonetic syllabaries are also used to indicate the pronunciation of *kanji* (since the ideograph gives no clue about how it should be pronounced).

China, in fact, has influenced Japan in more ways than can be listed here, but with respect to the spoken language, Chinese and Japanese are completely different.

How difficult a language is Japanese?

If you are born and grow up in Japan, it's as easy to speak Japanese as any other language one is born to. *Kanji,* though, takes much more time to learn than a language like English or French written in a more or less phonetic alphabet. High school graduates are expected to know about 2000 *kanji,* but those who are older and wiser will know many more. Because of the difficulty in learning to write it, Japanese is considered by the U.S.

State Department to be among the most difficult languages in the world.

Learning to speak Japanese as a foreign language is another matter. The sound system is not difficult—similar to Spanish, in fact, so that Spanish speakers of Japanese have less of an accent than English speakers. Word order is not so important as it is in English, and in many ways the language seems more consistent than others, including English. That's the good news. The bad news is that the levels of politeness, which we have seen are extremely important in Japanese social intercourse, are marked in speech so that different words are used depending upon the relationship with the person being addressed. In addition, unlike the French, who may act impatiently or even contemptuous toward a visitor who ought to but does not speak passable French, the Japanese generally do not expect *gaijin* to speak much Japanese. Moreover, there is strong sympathy with the difficulty of learning another language on the part of the Japanese, many of whom feel they should be better at English for having studied it six years in school. The result of all this is that even well intentioned and well motivated Americans often abandon their study of the language early on.

The fact is that it is not easy to start to learn Japanese, or any language, when one is trying to carry out a full work routine and adjust to all that is new in another culture. More and more Americans do speak Japanese, but most who do have studied it in schools prior to going to Japan to work. Americans going to Japan without language preparation should carry realistic expectations about what they can and cannot learn. Still, many may be able to learn more than they think.

How do the Japanese feel about Americans because of the war?

It is difficult to give a clear answer with confidence, since how people feel and how people act may be very different. Also, there are very different feelings depending upon the age of the person—as is the case in any country when it comes to remembering the war years. It is curious, though, that this is a concern of almost every American who visits Japan, and yet it is almost never an issue in interpersonal relations. (Mexicans may be more resentful over the U.S. taking so much of its land a century ago, but Americans rarely think to worry about that when they visit Mexico.)

If asked, some Japanese will tell you that the past is the past, that the war and its horrors suffered and inflicted have been dealt with, and that this is another era. Nearly all Japanese are strongly against Japan's becoming involved in any other war and, of course, the anti-nuclear sentiment is particularly strong in this, the only land to suffer—twice—as victims of the atomic bomb. But even here, emotion is directed against war and atomic weapons rather than the country that used the weapons.

There are other war-related memories that are still important in Japan, though most foreigners have little exposure to them. Some people dislike certain foods because they were all that was available during the occupation. Military songs are sometimes sung by wistful older men in bars late at night. Japanese feelings about America because of the war are not as resentful as Americans often imagine. In overt ways, at least, World War II is far more on the minds of Americans than Japanese.

Isn't Japan very crowded? I've seen pictures of people being crammed into subway cars.

Japan is one of the most densely populated countries in the world. The total land area of all the islands of Japan is roughly comparable to that of the state of California. Imagine 80% of this area being mountainous and unsuitable for farming, let alone urban development. Then populate the remaining 20% with half of the population of the United States, and you have an idea of the population density of Japan. Nearly a fourth of the Japanese, over thirty million, live in the greater Tokyo area—a megalopolis that includes the port of Yokohama, the industrial city of Kawasaki and other urban areas.

Because land is so precious, it is used with care and ingenuity. A department store utilizes not only every centimeter of interior floor space, it will also use the roof (typically for an amusement center, a nursery and pet shop) and extend, often, two, three or four floors under the ground.

The scale of things in Japan, however, is smaller than in the States. Streets are narrower, cars smaller, shops stock only a small quantity of each item instead of the large quantities seen in American stores, and so on. One learns to adjust to the difference in scale, especially since, even in Tokyo, one need walk only a short distance to escape from towering buildings and stroll through a quiet neighborhood of small wooden homes.

As for the famous "pushers" (*oshiya*) on the commuter trains, they do in fact pack the passengers in at a few of the busiest stations during rush hour, but it is usually possible to plan a schedule that will avoid the worst of rush hour crowding.

Isn't Japan the most expensive place in the world to live? I've heard steak costs $30.00 a pound.

Tokyo, at least, is usually near the top of those lists that tell which cities in the world have the highest costs of living. However, the range of costs is wide. Steaks, lobster, French wines—it is possible to pay very high prices for such items in Japan, but these are not by any means the typical Japanese fare.[4] There are simple excellent neighborhood restaurants where one can still get a complete tempura dinner for under $5.00—which is less than you would pay in the States. Anyone who is willing to get away from the expensive hotel and

[4] For anyone going to Japan, I strongly recommend *Eating Cheap in Japan,* available at any hotel or English language bookshop in Japan. It is a guide not to specific restaurants, but to the hundreds of food items available in tens of thousands of restaurants all over Japan. Even the first meal away from the tourist circuit will save more than the cost of the colorful guidebook. Kimiko Nagasawa and Camy Condon, *Eating Cheap in Japan* (Shufonotomo, 1974.)

restaurant area, and enter any of the consistently clean and good small Japanese restaurants, does not need to spend more in Japan than in the U.S.[5]

What about pollution? I've seen pictures of people wearing masks because of the bad air.

During its period of intense industrial and economic growth, Japan has polluted its beautiful rivers, hillsides and seas in a manner that is particularly shameful in a country that has always valued living in harmony with nature. There are some vigorous efforts to stop and reverse this pattern, however, and some cause for optimism.

Tokyo air quality has been improving each year for many years. The Japanese measure the number of days each year that Mt. Fuji can be seen from a particular point in Tokyo, and each year the number of days increases. People do not wear masks because of air pollution, however, though that erroneous image has found its way even into some social studies textbooks in the U.S. Many Japanese wear little gauze face masks, like doctors or nurses, when they have colds, and they wear them for typically Japanese reasons: not to avoid catching something, but to avoid causing others to catch their cold germs.

What about gift giving?

Gift giving in Japan reflects much of the culture and so is very different from gift giving in the States. Not only who gives gifts, but what kind of gifts are given, when they are given, and how they are given are all equally important. Acting inappropriately can confuse others and disrupt the very relationships that gifts are intended to reflect.

[5] Housing in Japan is expensive, depending upon what kind of accommodations a person wants. But there are still inns and hotels, clean and well located in Tokyo, that charge rates comparable to those in the States.

There are two big times a year when gifts are presented to those persons to whom an individual or a family feels a special enduring indebtedness: *Oseibo,* toward the end of the year, and *O-chugen,* at mid-year. At these times, for example, a married couple will give a gift to their *nakodo* (the go-between or matchmaker/marriage witness). People also give gifts to their doctors, music teachers, or others whom they wish to thank for past kindnesses and to anticipate continued kindness in the future. Some gifts are also presented to favored customers—at these times, even a nightclub hostess might give a small gift to a regular customer. These are also the times when huge bonuses are handed out—the economy swells with money and many large purchases, such as a car or a piano, might be made with the bonus money. Bonuses are calculated on the basis of salary and well understood in advance; there are no surprises in the bonus envelopes.

If you do go to a department store around gift giving time, you can get a good idea of what sorts of things are given. In the most popular price range, the gifts are usually practical items such as cooking oil or tea. You will also notice that the gift items are displayed not by kind of gift but by prices—¥5,000 items in one area, ¥10,000 in another, and so on. This is most instructive, for a gift given in Japan must be of the appropriate value for the particular relationship. It can be just as bad to spend too much on a gift as to spend too little—meanings will be read into the gift in either case. Fortunately or not, most foreigners in Japan do not get involved in this particular ritual gift giving practice.

There are other occasions for giving gifts in Japan, however, that an American will become involved in. When one is the personal guest of someone at a company, or when one visits someone's home, it is appropriate to bring a gift. A wedding invitation also calls for a gift, as does a visit to a funeral. Money is usually given in the latter case and very often for weddings, as well. Inquire of Japanese friends for what is appropriate.

There are a few basic considerations in selecting and presenting gifts. Americans going to Japan are likely to want to bring gifts that are uniquely American and not readily available in Japan. Regional folkcraft, a book of photographs, or certain attractively packaged regional food items are some possibilities. Do not give something that you or one of your friends have made, unless your artistic talents are widely valued. Japanese don't quite know how to respond to a pin cushion little Debbie made in sewing class.

Japanese like things that come in sets. This is apparent in stores where most gift items displayed contain several, usually three or five pieces. The number four (*shi*) has unpleasant associations with the Japanese word for death, and thus sets of four items are not appealing. You might keep all this in mind when making a selection.

As with everything in Japan, how something is done is as important as what is done; packaging matters very much. Gifts purchased in Japan are usually given with the store's wrapping paper still intact, for while department store paper may not be as elegant as paper that could be purchased separately, it does add the cachet of the store and any prestige that goes with it. (A friend once shocked a clerk at one of Tokyo's finest department stores by asking if he could purchase several yards of the store's paper for wrapping other gifts! No sale.)

When a gift is presented it will not be opened until later, away from the eyes of the giver. There are several reasons for this, including not wanting any tinge of disappointment or puzzlement on the face of the recipient to leak out; if several gifts are received, one also does not want to have comparisons made or duplications noticed. Gifts should be offered—and received—gracefully, with two hands, and the giver should make some modest comment about the gift ("It's really a very little thing . . .") and the receiver should make appropriate protestations of the "Oh, you really shouldn't have brought anything" sort.

One other kind of gift giving in Japan needs to be mentioned: the *omiage,* or token gift one brings home after being away on a trip. Japanese tourists spend more money on *omiage* to take to family members, friends, and office mates than they do on items for themselves. Every train station in Japan has a selection of such items from which travelers can select something for the people back home. A few even have items that appear to have come from elsewhere, in case the traveler forgot to get something when he was there.

For Americans who work with Japanese, the best kind of *omiage* is something that can be shared, such as cookies or crackers. If an American boss gives his secretary an *omiage* that cannot be shared, it can be embarrassing. Her preference is to be able to share her gift and not be singled out.

Keep in mind that gifts are expressions of relationships and quite literally tokens of gratitude. To spontaneously give a Japanese something because you just saw the item and thought the person would like it causes all sorts of confusion and usually requires the recipient to (1) figure out why the gift was given, and if there was some ulterior motive, (2) determine the approximate value of the gift, and (3) find something reasonably appropriate to give back in order to restore the balance. This error is repeated over and over by well-meaning foreigners. Sadly, when the Japanese recipient does give something in return—often within hours—the *gai-jin* is confused: "Why can't the Japanese just accept a token of friendship without always balancing the books?" Americans should take care not to upset the delicate balance in human relationships.

Appendix A

Useful Japanese Language Expressions

When meeting someone and in everyday interaction:

Hajimemashite I'm pleased to meet to meet you. (Only when meeting for the first time.)

Yoroshiku, onegai shimasu (A polite expression which is important in expressing your hope for a good relationship with the person you have met.)

Sumimasen (A humble expression which apologizes for any bother one may have caused—even when you are sure you didn't cause any bother.)

Arigatō gozaimasu "Thank you very much."

Dō itashimashite "You're welcome" (in response to "arigatō gozaimasu".)

sō desu (ne) (agreeing) "That's true, (isn't it)"; "That's right."

Arigatō gozaimashita - "Thank you very much." - for
Something that has been
Completed.

Ohayō gozaimasu   "Good morning."

Kon-nichiwa   "Good afternoon." (Any time from 10:00 a.m. until evening.)

Komban-wa   "Good evening."

When dining:

Kampai!   (The standard toast, with drinks, before beginning a meal.) "Cheers!"

Itadakimasu   (A polite expression said just before beginning a meal.)

Oishii (desu)   "Delicious"; (it's) "delicious."

dōzo   "Please have some . . ." "Please begin . . ." "Please go ahead . . ." etc.

dōmo   "Thank you" (in response to *dōzo*)

kekko desu   "That's enough"; "that's fine"; "no more, thank you," etc.

Gochisō-sama deshita   (A polite expression of appreciation to the host or hostess or cook, etc., after finishing a meal.)

Titles Within An Organization

These are a few representative, general titles. Different kinds of companies have different titles, so the reader is advised to learn the appropriate terminology for his or her kind of organization.

Kaicho   Chairman

Shacho   President

Fuku-Shacho   Vice President

Senmu-Torishimariyaku   Senior Executive Managing Director

Jomu-Torishimariyaku   Executive Managing Director

Torishimariyaku   Director

Bucho   Division Manager

Bucho Dairi   Deputy Division Manager

Kacho   Section Manager (Section Chief)

Kacho Dairi   Deputy Section Manager

Kakaricho   Chief

Appendix B

Recommended Readings

There are so many good books on Japan available today in English that it is difficult to select just a few. Two tips at the outset, though. If you have some hobby or special interest in a subject, look for books on that subject as it relates to Japan—crafts, music, theatre, sports, whatever. Any good bookstore which features books on and/or from Japan (the American branches of Maruzen and Kinokuniya may be the most complete) will have titles to intrigue and delight. Often the best route to understanding a culture is by way of some personal interest, particularly one that can be developed and discussed with the Japanese one meets. A Japanese executive who lived in the U.S. for many years recommends that in addition to reading books on Japan that are intended primarily for foreigners, it is also important to read what the Japanese themselves are reading. This is so that there can be something of mutual interest which can be discussed. It is not too difficult to find out which books available in English (usually originally in English and then translated into Japanese) are also popular in Japan. Sometimes a book originally published in the U.S. enjoys an even larger readership in Japanese translation; Ezra Vogel's book (below) is one such example.

Readers should not overlook Japanese fiction in translation, as scores of titles are widely available in inexpensive paperback books. Tuttle (Tokyo and Rutland, Vermont) probably publishes the largest selection of Japanese fiction in English translation. Yasunari Kawabata, who won the Nobel Prize in literature, and the late Yukio Mishima were among the most popular writers for American readers. An older work that many Japanese feel gives one of the most "Japanesey" views of human relations is Junichiro Tanizaki's classic, *The Makioka Sisters*.

For keeping up on what is happening, there are four daily newspapers published in Japan in English. That is more than in any American city. Each has not only Japanese and international news, but also news features, columns, and translations from items in the Japanese press. The parent companies for three of these, the *Asahi, Mainichi* and *Yomiyuri,* are the three major Japanese newspapers; the fourth, *The Japan Times,* is the largest of the English language papers.

There are also journals which publish translations of Japanese articles which are worth looking into, particularly *The Japanese Interpreter* and the *Japan Echo.*

Anyone visiting Japan must go browsing at one of the large Japanese bookstores. Not only will readers find a remarkably wide selection of books on Japan in English, they will also be able to observe what the Japanese readers are interested in today.

For Americans who wish to purchase Japanese books,

magazines and newspapers, two large Japanese bookstores, Maruzen and Kinokuniya, have branches in American cities with large Japanese populations such as Los Angeles, San Francisco and New York.

Here are a few books that should stimulate and inform:

Lewis Austin. *Saints and Samurai: The Political Culture of the American and Japanese Elites.* (New Haven: Yale University Press, 1975)   Though the titles may sound academic, this book, which is based on a study of leaders in both societies, offers lucid insights into comparative leadership styles of Japanese and Americans.

Jackson H. Bailey, editor. *Listening to Japan: A Japanese Anthology.* (New York: Praeger, 1973)   This is an excellent collection of articles written by Japanese on a broad range of cultural themes—values, politics, economics, hopes and fears.

Ronald Bell, editor. *The Japanese Experience.* (New York and Tokyo: Weatherhill, 1973)   A unique collection of interviews with foreigners, some noted and some unnoticed, who live in Japan. They give their impressions of the Japanese and how they feel about being foreigners in Japan.

John Condon and Keisuke Kurata. *In Search of What's Japanese about Japan.* (Tokyo: Shufunotomo, 1975)   Central values and cultural patterns that help shape the Japanese character illustrated with over 350 photographs and brief commentary.

Takie Sugiyama Lebra. *Japanese Patterns of Behavior.* (Honolulu: University of Hawaii Press, 1976) and Takie Sugiyama Lebra and William P. Lebra, editors. *Japanese Culture and Behavior.* (Honolulu: University of Hawaii Press, 1974)   The first book, authored by Professor Lebra, brings together considerable data and many theories into a cogent interpretation of Japanese behavior. The latter book is an excellent collection of articles and excerpts from leading social scientific writing on Japan today.

Fosco Maraini. *Japan: Patterns of Continuity.* (Tokyo: Kenkyusha, 1970)   An exquisite and very popular book of photographs with commentary on traditions and aesthetics in Japan by a noted Italian Japanologist.

Chie Nakane. *Japanese Society.* (Berkeley and Los Angeles: University of California Press, 1970)   The modern "classic" on the vertical society by one of Japan's leading anthropologists.

Edwin O. Reischauer. *The Japanese.* (Cambridge: The Belknap Press of Harvard University Press, 1977)   A monumental work by the Harvard historian and former ambassador to Japan.

Ezra Vogel. *Japan as Number One.* (New York: Harper, 1979)   Provocative, stimulating, and a number one best seller in Japanese translation. Professor Vogel examines what Americans can learn from the Japanese.